Sexuality Education in Postsecondary and Professional Training Settings

Sexuality Education in Postsecondary and Professional Training Settings

James W. Maddock, PhD
Editor

Routledge
Taylor & Francis Group
New York London

Sexuality Education in Postsecondary and Professional Training Settings has also been published as *Journal of Psychology & Human Sexuality*, Volume 9, Numbers 3/4 1997.

Cover design by Monica L. Seifert

First published by
The Haworth Press, Inc., 10 Alice Street, Binghamton, NY 13904-1580 USA

This edition published 2012 by Routledge

Routledge	Routledge
Taylor & Francis Group	Taylor & Francis Group
711 Third Avenue	2 Park Square, Milton
New York, NY 10017	Park, Abingdon, Oxon
	OX14 4RN

Library of Congress Cataloging-in-Publication Data

Sexuality education in postsecondary and professional training settings / James W. Maddock, editor.
    p. cm.
    Simultaneously published in the Journal of psychology & human sexuality, Vol. 9, No. 3/4, 1997.
    Includes bibliographical references and index.
    ISBN 0-7890-0027-X (alk. paper)
    1. Sex instruction. 2. Postsecondary education. I. Maddock, James W.
HQ57.3.S49 1997
613.9071–dc21   97-14977
                                                      CIP

ISBN 13: 978-0-7890-0027-9 (hbk)

Sexuality Education in Postsecondary and Professional Training Settings

CONTENTS

ABOUT THE EDITOR

James W. Maddock, PhD, is Professor of Family Social Science at the University of Minnesota, where he teaches and does research in the area of families and sexuality. He is also a licensed marriage and family therapist and is certified as a sex educator and sex therapist. Since 1970, he has been involved in sexuality education as a teacher, program developer, professional trainer, and consultant. Dr. Maddock has authored numerous articles and book chapters related to sexuality education, including co-editing *Human Sexuality and the Family* (The Haworth Press, 1983) and co-authoring, with his wife, *Incestuous Families: An Ecological Approach to Understanding and Treatment* (W. W. Norton, 1995). Previously, he served as the Director of Family Life Education for the Association for Family Living in Chicago and then as Education and Training Director for the Program in Human Sexuality at the University of Minnesota Medical School. Dr. Maddock is a former national president of the American Association of Sex Educators, Counselors, and Therapists.

Preface

The focus of this publication is on sexuality education in postsecondary educational settings; thus, it is primarily about educating young adults in contexts ranging from undergraduate courses to specialized medical or theological training. The articles deal with selected topics, and the authors do not attempt to exhaustively detail all issues confronting sexuality educators in their various contexts. Instead, the articles illustrate a variety of methods for examining the complex and controversial phenomena which typify the task of sexuality education.

This volume is distinctive not so much for its diversity as for its richness of perspective. The authors are experienced sexuality educators in a variety of settings. Most have been educators–and perhaps teachers of other sexuality educators–long enough to have lived through several "stages" of its development in the 20th century. Thus, this volume forms a sort of collection of accumulated "wisdom" about sexuality education, its possibilities, and its pitfalls. I hope each article will be carefully read and reflected on by those who are concerned about the future of sexuality education in North America and elsewhere on the threshold of the 21st century.

Most of the articles were originally presented in varying formats at the 1995 annual conference of the Midcontinent Region of the Society for the Scientific Study of Sexuality (SSSS), entitled "Educating about Sexuality," chaired by Walter Bockting. Here, some articles have been intentionally juxtaposed to help the reader compare their content and contemplate the issues they raise. As I finished editing this volume, I found myself wishing I could have

[Haworth co-indexing entry note]: "Preface." Maddock, James W. Co-published simultaneously in *Journal of Psychology & Human Sexuality* (The Haworth Press, Inc.) Vol. 9, No. 3/4, 1997, pp. xiii-xiv; and: *Sexuality Education in Postsecondary and Professional Training Settings* (ed: James W. Maddock) The Haworth Press, Inc., 1997, pp. xiii-xiv. Single or multiple copies of this article are available for a fee from The Haworth Document Delivery Service [1-800-342-9678, 9:00 a.m. - 5:00 p.m. (EST). E-mail address: getinfo@haworth.com].

xiii

assembled all the authors in one place for a week of intense discussion and debate about the current status of sexuality education and its future. I invite the reader to imagine, and join, such a dialogue.

My appreciation to all of the authors for their effort and cooperation, and a special thanks to Eli Coleman for his invitation, support, and patience in connection with developing this collection.

James W. Maddock, PhD

Sexuality Education:
A History Lesson

James W. Maddock, PhD

SUMMARY. Sexuality education is described as an ecological phenomenon, reflecting a variety of dialectical tensions in the context of
U.S. society. A brief overview of sexuality education highlights historical trends in the past century. After disclaiming the notion that
history repeats itself, I outline seven tentative "lessons," or guiding
principles, for planning future sexuality education efforts. *[Article
copies available for a fee from The Haworth Document Delivery Service:
1-800-342-9678. E-mail address: getinfo@haworth.com]*

We learn from history that we do not learn from history.

−G. F. W. Hegel

Taught in the traditional manner–a recitation of dates and facts
with no framework of meaning into which to place the information–
history can be extremely boring. Fortunately for sexuality educators, the subject matter has a certain inherent appeal. Even historical

James W. Maddock is affiliated with the Department of Family Social Science
at the University of Minnesota–Twin Cities.
Address correspondence to James W. Maddock, Department of Family Social
Science, 290 McNeal Hall - University of Minnesota, 1985 Buford Avenue,
St. Paul, MN 55108.

[Haworth co-indexing entry note]: "Sexuality Education: A History Lesson." Maddock, James W.
Co-published simultaneously in *Journal of Psychology & Human Sexuality* (The Haworth Press, Inc.)
Vol. 9, No. 3/4, 1997, pp. 1-22; and: *Sexuality Education in Postsecondary and Professional Training
Settings* (ed: James W. Maddock) The Haworth Press, Inc., 1997, pp. 1-22. Single or multiple copies of
this article are available for a fee from The Haworth Document Delivery Service [1-800-342-9678, 9:00
a.m. - 5:00 p.m. (EST). E-mail address: getinfo@haworth.com].

1

trivia about sex can be fascinating to students of any age. How many average citizens–or even professional educators–have had an opportunity to thoroughly study the history of a society or a culture via its sexual attitudes and practices? Yet, once sensitized to the issues, sex-related issues can be recognized as embedded in many historical trends as well as in current events that are "making history" for future generations.

In this article, I will attempt to provide some guidelines by which a framework of meaning for understanding sexuality education can be constructed. Then I will consider certain events from the perspective of that framework. Finally, I will attempt to draw a few "lessons from history" that might be helpful in understanding present and future trends in sexuality education.

BACKGROUND

Every effort to derive meaning from history requires a certain amount of "existential stage-setting" (Kaplan, 1964). To differentiate the approach taken in this article from others that are possible, the philosophical assumptions that guide my understanding of history as an aspect of human experience need to be made explicit. Taken together, they comprise a framework I have labeled "dialectical ecology" (Maddock, 1993):

- "Reality" is constituted by the transactions between systems and environments; that is, relationships make things what they are.
- Life is always in the process of *becoming*; that is, change is inherent in the universe.
- Humans simultaneously perceive *and* create their worlds; put another way, they co-construct the world in dialogue with what actually exists.
- Every system is both a subsystem to the systems that surround it and an ecosystem to the systems that comprise it; therefore, the fundamental unit of reality is the *subsystem/ecosystem relationship,* or the system-in-transformation.
- The study of human history involves the construction of *meaning* about events in the past, guided by *present* experience.

MAJOR DIALECTICAL DIMENSIONS

The cultural context of contemporary sexuality education in North America reflects (a) a fundamental shift in gender relations (increasingly, a global phenomenon); (b) a substantial and enduring *ambivalence* toward erotic expression (more than most cultures of the world); (c) transformation into a pangeographic digitalized economy; (d) rapid globalization of communication, information, and technology; (e) a global context of geopolitical destabilization and cultural diversification (characterized by conflict between large and small geopolitical entities as well as dissension between individuals and groups). Within this complex cultural ecology, sexuality in contemporary North American society reflects a variety of inherent (dialectical) tensions, recognition of which is important to understanding the twentieth century history of sexuality education:

- Tension between sexuality as good and sexuality as evil.
- Tension between individual freedom and social order.
- Tension between masculinization and feminization of sexuality.
- Tension between conformity and diversity in sexual expression.
- Tension between sexuality information as power and sexuality information as control.
- Tension between eroticism as pleasure and eroticism as danger.
- Tension between sexuality education for competence and sexuality education for safety.
- Tension between traditionalism and progressivism with regard to sexual attitudes and ethics.
- Tension between sexuality as public concern and sexuality as private experience.

To appreciate the impact of these influences, one needs to recognize *both* the tension *and* the complementarity between their apparent polarities. In ecological terms, the patterns of relationship between subsystems and ecosystems over time are the basis for deriving the meaning of history. Put more simply, any given event should be interpreted in light of the larger context that surrounds it, while avoiding the temptation to use the context to causally explain the event. This is the paradox that underlies Hegel's observation cited at the beginning of this article: Humans construct the meaning of history as part of the process of experiencing the present that the past has produced; thus, there can be no real "learning" from history, since each present moment is unique and brings with it a new understanding of the past. History does not repeat itself; therefore, the lessons of history must be continuously relearned under ever-changing circumstances, that is, in the *emerging present*.

At the same time, framing history as an ecological dialectic can guide present understanding and behavior based upon the recognition of the interconnectedness of all life processes and all events (Bateson, 1972; Naess, 1989). Just as a single act of dropping trash at the side of a road can affect the lives of subsequent travelers, so the behavior of each individual and each group within a particular social context influences the history in which others will someday find meaning–and, hopefully, wisdom.

HISTORICAL OVERVIEW

The overview that follows should be recognized as reflecting "eth-class" phenomena (cf., D'Emilio & Freedman, 1988; Foucault, 1978; Graham, 1992; Johnson, 1994; Lister, 1986; Money, 1985; Sears, 1992). That is, the historical phenomena mentioned were not characteristic of every group; nevertheless, together they comprised a kind of cultural atmosphere that affected every citizen to some degree, if only by creating images that, in turn, produced pressure to conform.

The sexual climate that has predominated in the United States (and Canada, to a considerable extent) through the twentieth century is substantially rooted in the social, political, and economic order of eighteenth century Europe, reflecting some of the same forces that impelled the European migration to North America. Arriving in what was for them a "New World," Europeans often took lands and lives from the native populations and, in return, brought new technology to "tame" the land and "civilize" the people; new religious beliefs and customs that offered a better life in the hereafter while simultaneously shaming and restricting natives' habits and lifestyles; and new diseases–including sexually transmitted diseases– that sometimes decimated local populations.[1]

Native sexual beliefs and customs were among the first things to be altered by pressure from European settlers. In addition, clashes between various groups with European origins had implications for sexuality. The Judaeo-Christian tradition of Western Europe arrived in the Americas in at least three broad forms. One was the Roman Catholic mysticism of the Spanish *conquistadores,* whose influence combined with native Indian religions and spread through South and Central Americas into the southern United States. The second was the liberal rationality of the Deists, among whom were many of the earliest political leaders who shaped the original Federation of States, and under whom religious freedom was constitutionally established. The third was the pietism (personal holiness) best represented by the Puritans, who separated from the Church of England seeking religious freedom in America–but only for themselves. Their local communities in the New England colonies publicly tortured citizens and burned witches at the stake for heretical beliefs and supposed moral crimes, many of which were distinctly sexual in nature.[2]

As the European population of the so-called New World grew, these three influences were increasingly juxtaposed, sometimes creatively, often destructively. The tensions that arose have survived to the present day in the U.S., mirrored in such controversial social issues as abortion, pornography, gender roles, individual sexual rights–and sexuality education (Bullough, 1976; Bullough & Bullough, 1977; D'Emilio & Freedman, 1988; Money, 1985; Reiss & Reiss, 1990; Richardson, 1971).

The "high culture" atmospheres of Western Europe and the United States were notably similar during the 1800s, even though historical events in these regions differed significantly. In the U.S., a frontier mentality predominated as the continent was settled from east to west by successive waves of immigrants, primarily from Europe. Emphasis was on individual freedom and pragmatic necessity, although these were somewhat tempered by the spirit of Protestant revivalism that accompanied the migration across the country. Brothels were common; women were sometimes sold–or sold themselves–as wives; slaves were used for sexual purposes as well as for labor. Yet "sexual purity," marriage, and monogamy were held out as ideals for all, rooted in a God-given order.

As immigration and economic changes brought more and more people into large cities and created the social problems that accompanied the Industrial Revolution of the late nineteenth century, a pattern of morality emerged that was named for England's Queen Victoria. Victorianism dictated strict codes for family values, relations between men and women, and sexual behavior. Narrowly defined moralistic attitudes dominated people's lives. Even those who did not conform to the rules knew exactly what rules they were choosing to disobey. Much of American society was characterized by a kind of sexual hysteria. Modesty was emphasized in order to avoid unleashing rampant passions. Masturbation was thought to cause serious illness or insanity, and extreme measures ranging from chastity belts to surgical cauterization were used to discourage children from touching their genitals. By the end of the 19th century, the so-called "Victorian" values and attitudes largely characterized life in the educated and privileged classes that dominated U.S. culture. These stressed individualism (thrift, hard work, and prudent investment) and distinct gender roles reflecting the division between work and family life (and the accompanying distinction between "good" and "bad" women). The lives of many did not conform to these ideals–particularly among the lower classes in urban areas and isolated towns in the rural West, as well as among New England Shakers, polygamous Mormons, and "free love" groups. Nevertheless, everyone had a fairly clear notion of the idealized version of life, that is, what *ought* to be the standards of behavior (and what evils might befall those who did not live up to them).

In this cultural context, the roots of formal sexuality education outside of the family were embedded in the influences of rapid urbanization and industrialization. Churches and quasi-religious organizations such as the YMCA and YWCA responded to changing social conditions with programs of hygiene education–personal, social, and moral–a major target of which were various sexual practices. Special organizations such as the American Society for Social and Moral Prophylaxis were founded to coordinate nationwide educational efforts. These early attempts at sexuality education were authoritarian and moralistic, warning of the dire consequences of sexual indulgence (Money, 1985; Reiss & Reiss, 1990; Strong, 1972; Young, 1964).

Another influence on sexuality education was the emphasis on birth control emerging from the work of Margaret Sanger and others around the turn of the century. Besides providing a cornerstone for the development of feminist ideas and political action, Sanger and her colleagues gave an enormous boost to the legitimacy of sexuality apart from its reproductive consequences. However, the major focus of sexuality education until after World War I continued to be problem-centered—the personal and social hygiene that would combat prostitution, illegitimacy, and sexually transmitted diseases. So it might be said that sexuality education in the U.S. in the latter part of the nineteenth and early twentieth centuries consisted primarily of "authoritarian moralism," the goal of which was safety for an idealized family unit and protection for an idealized economic order.

The post-World War I era brought to the United States the writings of Sigmund Freud (and his emphasis on "natural" childhood sexuality), as well as a surge in nonmarital sex (and sexually transmitted diseases) that set the stage for a period that has come to be known as the "Roaring Twenties." Following World War I, the sexuality education focus could be characterized as "liberated" social hygiene information. Some of the moral emphases were set aside in favor of a more pragmatic approach to dealing with problems of sexuality. Between the two world wars, a whole new understanding of human sexuality emerged, rooted in Freudian theories of child development and the growing field of learning psychology in the U.S. Gradually, the emphasis on sexual restraint shifted from a moral to a psychological base. That is, it was recognized that sexual education was relevant for children only as long as it was appropriate to their particular stage of psychosexual development. According to Freudian theory, the apparently fragile childhood psyche is protected from undue emphasis on sex by the so-called "latency period," a lengthy time in middle childhood where there are supposedly no sexual interests or inclinations. Thus, the processes of sexuality education were tied more tightly to the family unit, since the concept of latency provided a rationale for the schools to refrain from involvement other than providing information on basic biology and on practical matters of bodily health and hygiene as children grew into adolescence (a rationale still used today by many of those opposing elementary school programs of sexuality education). However, with the continuously changing social conditions of the pre-World War II years, some sensed that a more positive approach to marriage, family life, and sexuality education was needed–and that the schools might, indeed, have a potential role to play.

Although hard times of economic depression and growing anxiety about world events dampened the personal and sexual freedoms that characterized the collapse of Victorianism, the social control of individual sexual expression continued to *lessen* steadily over each succeeding decade from the 1920s on–of course, more for males than for females. Freudian notions of sexuality (along with Krafft-Ebing's writings) influenced not only clinical work on sexual psychopathology, but filtered into the culture as part of the more general understanding of "normal" and "abnormal" sexual expression.

Everyday life in the United States was in certain ways suspended by the entry of the country into a second world war. While sex didn't disappear, men did. And women went to work in factories–disrupting marital routines, sexual activity, and the birth rate. But the most pressing issues of sexuality education were exported to the European and Asian theaters of war, in an effort to combat the inevitable surges in sexually transmitted diseases that accompany mobile populations and widespread prostitution.

The end of the War brought, for some, a return to normalcy, including sex and babies (a regular "baby boom," as Americans are continuously reminded); for others, it brought alienation and divorce (the 1946 divorce rate was not surpassed until 1974); for still others, a variety of problems, including the importation of "venereal diseases" from former battle zones abroad. Educators were mobilized to help combat this rise, as well as to deal with the personal and marital adjustment problems that had arisen within a nation at war. The high divorce rate gave further impetus to the development of comprehensive new "family life education" programs.

Another post-War event had a strong impact on sexuality and sex education in the U.S. The monumental sociological studies by Alfred Kinsey and his colleagues revealed patterns of sexual behavior that actually existed in the United States (Kinsey, Pomeroy, & Martin, 1948; Kinsey, Pomeroy, Martin, & Gebhard, 1953). Kinsey's work signaled the beginning of more public discussion of sexuality, as well as greater tolerance by many Americans of sexual practices that differed from their own.

From the end of World War II through the 1950s, the number of "personal hygiene," "preparation for marriage" and "family living" classes increased steadily. Improving the quality of family life began to be touted as one of the nation's top priorities, even though the characteristics of the ideal family continued to be narrowly defined. Gradually, a network of family-related courses evolved in the nation's high schools, and even in colleges and universities. Their emphasis was on middle-class values, particularly on adjustment to family roles and relationships, and on conformity to certain societal expectations. Sexuality issues were included, but usually in a disguised or indirect fashion. Obliquely transmitted information on developmental changes of puberty and basic reproductive processes was provided–though it was often "too little and too late." This information was made available primarily to females, both because education about menstruation afforded a more reliable excuse for providing some sex-related information and because most of the family life education occurred in home economics programs at various educational levels–although biology teachers and health educators (often athletic coaches) were recruited as well.

Relatively few teachers or educator groups were outspoken enough to risk offending public dignity by talking directly about the specifics of erotic behavior and reproduction, except under carefully controlled circumstances. The basic emphasis of family life education at the time was on "wholesomeness." Young people were encouraged to be respectful and cautious about sexual activity as well as concerned about the possible consequences for their personal adjustment and the welfare of their dating partners–along with the traditional worry about pregnancy and disease. All in all, it was a considerably more reasoned approach to guiding youth than had been the case in previous decades, although it was still largely predicated on fear and/or guilt (cf., Duvall, 1950, 1957, 1965; Kirkendall, 1961; Lorand, 1965; Pemberton, 1957).

Acceptance of diversity in sexual behavior grew subtly but persistently throughout the 1950s and 1960s. Actually, it was an extension of the trends begun after World War I, although such trends were far from a straight line rise–nor were they in any way uniform throughout the society (D'Emilio & Freedman, 1988; Reiss, 1960, 1986). However, one trend was both dramatic and extensive: Sex went *public* in a major way, swept along by technological advances, especially television and movies. When it came to social attitudes, the steady sexual *evolution* of the first half of this century became the sexual *revolution* of the 1960s. Not only were a significant number of individuals behaving at odds with social convention, they were willing to acknowledge–even flaunt–the fact that their personal sexual mores were considerably different from the recognized sexual attitudes and ethics of the larger society. No longer were most young people willing to give even lip service to Victorian attitudes toward sex. Even the "double standard" began to erode.

Changes in sexual attitudes were paralleled by changes in sexual information, which also served to focus public attention on sexuality. The laboratory studies of human sexual response by William Masters and Virginia Johnson (1966) created both curiosity and controversy. What is important to note here is not the findings themselves, but the very fact that such studies were able to be conducted and published. They had an enormous impact upon the climate of sexual research in the United States and, subsequently, upon the sexual attitudes and expectations of American citizens. After Kinsey and Masters and Johnson, human sexuality could be studied scientifically and talked about publicly–in fact, endlessly in the media–and services could be offered to solve sexual problems and improve sexual satisfaction.

In this atmosphere, no longer could "family life education" be used as a polite euphemism for sexuality education. Students would not be satisfied with rainy day lectures from the football coach (boys only), or by viewing Walt Disney's "Story of Menstruation" (girls only). Social scientists and educators finally acknowledged openly what many of them had known all along: In order to be effective, sexuality educators have to deal with actual behavior and feelings, as well as biological facts and social statistics. Growing numbers claimed sexual expression to be one of the inherent rights of individuals, even protected by the U.S. Constitution. Against this background, a small number of determined professionals began the difficult task of making sexuality a truly legitimate subject of education in the nation's schools by creating in 1964 a resource and advocacy organization known as the Sex Information and Education Council of the United States (SIECUS). Just three years later, another network of individuals founded the American Association of Sex Educators and Counselors (AASEC), a membership and training organization for professionals.

As might have been anticipated, the nation was not fully ready to embrace sexuality and rally to the cause of sex education. To the contrary, the attempts to confront sexual problems head-on produced strong opposition, and sex education in the schools joined race, war, and poverty as a major social issue of the decade. In many communities, national organizations such as the John Birch Society and the Christian Crusade formed front groups that pledged to reveal sex education in school classrooms as an organized communist conspiracy.[3] Battle lines were drawn. For a time during the mid-sixties, federal and state support for family life and sex education was fairly visible in the form of Title III money for supplies such as audiovisual materials and special grants for teacher training and demonstration projects. This support rapidly dwindled, however, due to political changes, shifting priorities, and perhaps also to the heat of the sex education controversy–which meant that some voters could be alienated.

The conflict reached perhaps its highest pitch in 1967-1969, when hardly a day passed without some mention of the controversy in the national media (Breasted, 1970). For example, on what must have been a slow news day in mid-July, 1968, the headline of the *Chicago Sunday Tribune* announced: **RED SEX PLOT BARED**, and front-page stories and editorial commentaries filled the edition. During those years, school board elections were often won or lost on the basis of a candidate's stand on sex education. When the dust finally settled, the results were mixed. In some communities, the well-organized and well-financed right-wing extremists had persuaded the majority of parents to abandon existing school sexuality education programs, or even to pass legislation forbidding the future creation of such programs. For example, the California state legislature passed a bill specifically forbidding the use of any SIECUS-related materials in state classrooms–shortly after SIECUS had worked closely with a publisher on a comprehensive and expensive sexuality education program utilizing filmstrips and audiotapes. In other locations, school districts decided not to risk outright confrontation; they shelved their curriculum plans for the time being, or they quietly inserted some minimal material at strategic points in existing biology, health, or home economics courses. A few brave school officials in particular communities simply weathered the storm and depended on the basic good will of parents for eventual support. Similarly, a small number of courageous teachers prepared themselves through reading and training programs. They introduced units or entire courses into their classrooms, and they held class discussions and answered students' questions openly and honestly, thereby risking the wrath of parents–and their jobs. In the end, many of these administrators and teachers were vindicated, and they won the support of parents in local communities, as well as occasional legal battles.

This proved to be a pattern that persisted for nearly two decades. The eruption of a major controversy over sexuality education sometimes resulted in restricting or abolishing a particularly comprehensive (and often high quality) program. Almost anyone who has been doing sexuality education for a number of years can cite examples of this. Overall, however, the amount of sexuality education provided by schools across North America actually continued to *grow,* at virtually all educational levels. For the most part, this growth was slow and unobtrusive. When a particular community took a close look at the issue of school sexuality education programs, it most often ended up *increasing* its efforts–although the program might omit or minimize topics that many professional sexuality educators tend to see as important, such as masturbation, contraception, or gay/lesbian issues, to name a few.

The decade of the 1970s was a period of expansion and consolidation in many areas of sexuality education. First of all, it could now be referred to directly–there was no longer the need to use the "family life education" euphemism to disguise the fact that sexuality education was occurring. Particularly noticeable at the beginning of the decade was the lack of trained educators and other professionals who were qualified to teach sexuality education. This resulted in a tremendous effort to provide such training, and sexuality education for health and helping professionals was one of the hallmarks of the decade. During this period, AASEC (now AASECT) grew from a small, struggling group of specialists to a flourishing organization that provided training and certification in sex education as well as sex counseling and sex therapy. SIECUS developed a full-scale publishing and information dissemination program that reached into every corner of the U.S., spawned a parallel organization in Canada, and drew requests for resource help from countries throughout the world. Interest in sex research grew as well, and concern about the role of sexuality in higher education produced a rapid growth in a specialized organization, the Society for the Scientific Study of Sexuality (SSSS). At one point, both SSSS and AASECT examined the possibilities for accrediting institutional training in sex-related research and education, though such efforts were shelved when they proved to be extremely costly, legally risky, and bureaucratically complex.

In addition to these ongoing efforts to broaden and deepen sexuality education, some other trends of the 1970s are noteworthy. One was the official recognition by the World Health Organization (WHO, 1975)[4] that SIECUS was correct–sexuality is an aspect of health that needs to be nurtured and promoted. Another important component of that decade was the increased visibility of women's issues in society, spurred by the rhetoric of "Women's Liberation" and the feminist voices of the day. Gender issues began to creep into sexuality education, although attention to them was spotty at best; like sexuality education itself, they stirred up controversy and reactionary responses in a number of quarters. Third, the societal dynamics of the 1970s brought to the foreground issues of sexual pluralism. The civil rights emphasis of the 1960s was well-suited for use in the arena of sexuality, and groups of sexually disenfranchised people made a bid for recognition, including acknowledgment of the need for sexuality education for themselves–ranging from those with physical and mental disabilities (as they were then known) to gay and lesbian individuals to those with specialized erotic interests such as sadomasochism. Fourth, an important but two-edged influence on sexuality education came to widespread public attention in the 1970s–the phenomenon of sex therapy. While the "new sex therapy" and the "new sex education" were complementary in many ways–sharing the spotlight of widespread public attention–they were also competitors for the interests of the public, the allegiance of professionals, and the financial support of government and other cultural institutions. The remedial possibilities of brief sex therapy became so popular that they soon overshadowed the efforts at prevention, including the interests and activities of social service and helping professionals themselves. Like other phenomena in U.S. society, the support of remedies for actual social problems has far exceeded the support of preventive efforts for potential social problems. All in all, however, the 1970s was a fast-paced decade that saw sexuality education come into its own in North America. No longer could it be seen as an esoteric phenomenon or as a foreign conspiracy (particularly since the "cold war" was beginning to thaw).

The politics and policies of the 1980s were experienced by many in the social/behavioral sciences, education, and helping professions–including sexual educators–as a kind of "hitting the brake" in an effort to stop the momentum of societal change achieved during the activist 1960s and 1970s. It is easy to blame right-wing political extremism–symbolized by the election of Ronald Reagan as U.S. President–for the rapid deceleration; there is some truth to this view, since sex education has long been a favorite target of the political Right. However, the situation was more complex. Sexuality education was embedded in a fabric of social change that began to be torn into small pieces by the very groups who had once worked together to weave it. Public supporters of sexuality education, and professionals working in the field, began to recognize that they did not always have the same allegiances or agendas. Across North America, the confrontation with the reality of pluralism–the very pluralism that sexuality educators claimed to support–began to fragment. Perhaps the most visible issue was the politics of gender equity and their impact on the entire culture. Other issues of civil rights and social diversity could remain academic or be confronted in compartmentalized ways or even be swept under the carpet. Gender issues, however, were pervasive, and they could not be readily escaped when the majority of the population was "sleeping with the enemy."

Similar splintering occurred throughout society as the U.S. and Canada began to struggle with the realities of cultural pluralism in a new way. For example, sexually disenfranchised groups that in earlier years had demanded sexuality education for themselves now demanded sexuality education *about* themselves for others. Family life educators discovered that the family forms they were working to support differed, depending upon their own values, attitudes, and backgrounds. Sexuality educators were confronted by resistance and hostility among groups they had been trying to help, when the subtle social and political agendas around racism, sexism, homophobia, and other -isms began to be identified. Simply put, the relationship between sexuality and *social power* began to be highlighted, along with the differing value assumptions of groups within an increasingly diverse society. Suddenly, what had previously appeared to be morally grounded, high-minded, and well-intentioned efforts at education about human sexuality began to be challenged.

At this point, two other phenomena entered the picture, and each has had an enormous impact upon sexuality education in North America. The first was the identification of the HIV virus and a resultant recognition that sexually transmitted diseases were no longer just inconvenient, embarrassing, or painful, but could be incurable and lethal. The second was the increasing public awareness of sex-related violence–not as an instance of rare, exotic behavior by a handful of "perverts," but as an everyday occurrence involving familiar people in familiar places such as homes, schools, offices, factories, and public recreation areas.

Just when many sexology professionals thought that momentum had been gained toward a positive basis for sexuality education and an open exploration of sexual potential, sexuality was once again cast in the role of risk and menace in the public mind. In a sense, the 1980s did, indeed, continue the earlier focus on sexuality as a health entity; however, once again it was cast in a negative light like that of the Victorian period–sex as a "public health hazard." As a result, the motivation for providing sexuality education has again become safety-oriented and moralistic. Against the background of cultural diversity and factionalism identified above, sexuality education continues to be a major challenge as it seeks to find some broad base of support despite the dynamics of alienation and blame among various groups in society. Some examples: The genders appear to be at war on many fronts. Efforts at contraceptive education are viewed as genocidal by certain ethnic groups. A sizable portion of the heterosexual population blame the "gay/lesbian counterculture" for the spread of AIDS and other diseases, as well as the "seduction" of youth into "alternative lifestyles." Abortion is viewed as a form of villainous "murder" by certain religiously affiliated groups. Some politicians accuse family educators and other professionals of promoting the breakdown of "traditional family values."

What history is being constructed in the 1990s is not yet known. It is too close to permit a clear perspective on its meaning and significance. One thing is certain, however; history is being remade in shorter and shorter time frames, so that the luxury of time for reflection and learning is disappearing. Perhaps one short-term observation is worth making: At this point in time, North Americans appear to be sharply divided on major sex-related issues; the U.S. and Canada have become polarized societies. Extremism characterizes much of the debate. There is strong support for both conservative and liberal orientations—with each viewpoint claiming to reflect the majority—while a shrinking number of citizens struggles to cling to middle ground. Certain of these divergent views are religiously based, for example, the opposition to free choice about abortion. Other issues are characterized more by subjective opinion and/or practical arguments, for example, the debate over the connection between pornography and sexual violence. In a recent national survey conducted by the Kinsey Institute for Sex Research (Reinisch & Beasley, 1990), more than half the respondents "flunked" an eighteen-question test on basic sexual physiology and behavior. What does this say about the success of sexuality education efforts to date?

LESSONS FROM HISTORY

Despite the truth of Hegel's comment with which this article begins, history is all that humans have to teach them about life.

What has gone before inevitably shapes what comes after; however, it is just as true that what happens in the present *reshapes* human understanding of what has gone before. With these stipulations, I will conclude by suggesting several ways in which the foregoing historical observations can helpfully inform present understanding of sexuality education.

First, sexuality education needs to be recognized as only a particular case of a more general issue characterizing human experience. Beneath the problems of providing sexuality education lies the universal power struggle between parents and children, old and young, teachers and pupils. The general language and tone of every discourse about sexuality is that the wise elders know the "truth" and want to guide their children in avoiding the dangers of life. However, in light of postmodern communications technology, every belief about what is true and important is challenged radically and continuously by the rapid pace of social transformation. Therefore, the most important truths that older generations have to offer younger generations are guidelines for how to find their own way in an evolving world of increasing complexity–characterized by a considerable amount of uncertainty and chaos.

Second, the United States and Canada are not now–nor have they ever been–homogeneous "melting pots" of ethnic identities, cultural values, and social attitudes. Rather, North American history is characterized by conflict, and by attempts to balance among various ideas and influences. Nowhere is this more striking than in relation to sexuality. Yet, it has been an equally big mistake for sexuality educators and other self-identified political liberals to foster the notion that the ethnic and/or sexual identity of individuals can be achieved without regard to their consequences for the society as a whole. Individual rights do need to be balanced with concern for the common good. The mixture of dogmatic rhetoric on civil rights and the traditional U.S. overemphasis on individual freedom has eroded the dialectical balance of individual and community and has created a toxic recipe for self-justifying violence.[5]

Third, the *family* is inevitably the primary source of sexuality education for children.[6] For some time, it has been recognized that sexuality education occurs in close relationships even if adults are not aware of providing it. The nature of everyday behavior in fami-

lies is such that children will inevitably absorb meanings and attitudes regarding both gender and erotic aspects of sexuality. The
degree of respect shown to female and male family members has a
particularly strong impact upon the emerging gender identities of
children. Similarly, the family's appreciation of embodiment, including positive forms of touch and facilitation of appropriate erotic
expression, contributes to the personality development and self-
image of the young members. Therefore, all forms of sexuality
education ought to be done *in coordination with* families rather than
viewed as substitutes for what families are not doing.

Fourth, there is a reason why sexuality education is controversial
and will inevitably continue to be. Attitudes toward sexuality reflect
fundamental existential issues: What is life all about? What are the
fundamental components of human nature? What are the goals of a
society? What do present generations hope to pass on to future
generations? These are not easy matters upon which to agree. Further, in the process of social evolution, today's heresies easily become tomorrow's truths.

Fifth, even if goals for sexuality education could be broadly
agreed upon–beyond eliminating problems such as unplanned pregnancy or STDs–there is still very little data to support its effectiveness; at least, effectiveness measured in cold, hard, scientific terms
known as "outcome data." Often, sexuality educators have es-
poused lofty goals, made promises to reach them, and then failed by
most standards. In the world of post-positivist science, *understanding* of phenomena is becoming more important than prediction and
control. What, then, should be revised–goals, or the means to achieve
them? Some years ago, the widely publicized Mathtech Research
Report on sexuality education put it bluntly:

> Advocates of sex education courses have established for
> themselves a truly formidable task. They have described many
> goals for sex education programs, including changes in the
> students' knowledge, attitudes about sexual matters, self-per-
> ceptions, decision-making skills, communication skills, other
> interpersonal skills, fears, and social and sexual behaviors. In
> some cases, changes in the frequency of particular types of
> behavior are sought. In other cases, changes in the quality of

behavior are sought. For example, it is hoped that sex education will facilitate rewarding sexual expression, tolerant behavior, successful decision-making, and satisfying interpersonal
relationships. These goals are extremely demanding, and in many
respects, it is unfair to judge sex education programs by the
degree to which they meet all of these goals.

The ambitiousness of these goals can be demonstrated by
comparing them to the goals of other courses. In many classes,
the goals include the increase in knowledge of particular topics (e.g., American history) or the improvement in specific
academic skills (e.g., reading or math). Rarely do the goals of
other courses include changes in attitudes, interpersonal skills,
or nonacademic behavior. (Kirby, 1984, p. 10)

Sixth, perhaps the most powerful contributor to contemporary
change around the globe is communications technology. The so-
called "Digital Age" is dawning, and Marshall McLuhan (1965)
was right: The medium *is* the message. The density and rapidity of
feedback on ideas, feelings, behavior, and political activities, as
well as information and images related to commercial products, is
mindboggling. Recognition is growing that the technology that was
predicted to bring all people of the world together may instead be
driving human groups further apart. When people in countries with
few resources are bombarded daily with images of people in countries that have many resources–and squander them–the result is
distance and alienation. When people can live their lives in "virtu-
al reality"–devoid of face-to-face and skin-to-skin contact, but
stimulated by artificial means–then dehumanization is an inevitable result, and attachment and love will suffer. Although a vibrator
can be a valuable marital aid, and a computer bulletin board a
helpful place to find a date, sexual technology must remain in the
service of *human* sexuality, balanced by wisdom and a sense of
ethics.

A final lesson: The challenge is fundamentally an ecological one.
I am firmly convinced that *ecological balancing* is the key variable
in the future of sexuality education. Dialectical synthesis is the
ongoing act of transforming all of the tensions that characterize
sexuality. Ultimately, it is not a question of whether the changes will

occur; what matters is *how* the inescapable transformations are accomplished. Just as the entire universe is reflected in a drop of water, so are all possibilities for being human reflected in a single transaction between persons. More important than grand goals are ethical actions on a moment-by-moment basis. Sexuality educators should make ample use of the resources of the world and of human experience. Over time, scholars and researchers in the sexual sciences come to know a secret: Artists, writers, poets, and story-tellers have always done the best job of teaching humans about sexuality, for they share their experience and their wisdom unfettered by some of the artificial demands of "scientific credibility." *For sexuality educators and other sexology professionals, this may be the most important history lesson of all.*

NOTES

1. These comments are not intended to imply a belief in American Indians as "noble savages," creators of a simple, idyllic culture without violence or any type of sexual distortion. Rather, I intend to highlight the Eurocentrism that characterized the eighteenth century immigration to North America, including certain sex-related attitudes and values.

2. French Catholicism also had an impact as Europeans settled North America. However, its influence was primary and lasting across eastern and central Canada, while it was gradually confined to isolated areas of the United States.

3. The former Soviet Union's leading sexologist, Igor Kon, has revealed that, during the Cold War years, citizens in his country were warned against sexuality education as an "Imperialist Western plot to undermine the morals of Soviet youth" (Kon, 1988; Maddock & Kon, 1994).

4. The WHO Task Force defined *sexual health* as: "the integration of the somatic, emotional, intellectual, and social aspects of sexual being, in ways that are positively enriching and that enhance personality, communication, and love" (1975, p. 6).

5. Similar issues exist regarding the status and role of Quebec as a province, and a "culture," within the nation of Canada.

6. By "family," I refer to whatever grouping of individuals composes the primary social context of support and meaning-making for children and youth as well as for adults. While hereditary kinship needs to be acknowledged as a primary form of family connection, recognition should also be given to all of the ways in which families are formed by intentional choice and/or designated by community custom.

REFERENCES

Bateson, G. (1972). *Steps to an ecology of mind*. New York: Ballantine.

Breasted, M. (1970). *Oh! Sex education!* New York: Praeger.

Bullough, V. (1976). *Sexual variance in society and history*. New York: Wiley.

Bullough, V., & Bullough, B. (1977). *Sin, sickness, and sanity*. New York: New American Library.

D'Emilio, J., & Freedman, E. (1988). *Intimate matters: A history of sexuality in America*. New York: Harper & Row.

Duvall, E. (1950, 1957). *Facts of life and love for teenagers* (rev. ed., 1957). New York: Association Press.

Duvall, E. (1965). *Why wait till marriage?* New York: Association Press.

Foucault, M. (1978). *The history of sexuality, Vol. 1* (trans. by R. Hurley). New York: Pantheon.

Graham, S. (1992). "Most of the subjects were white and middle class": Trends in published research on African Americans in selected APA journals, 1970-1989. *American Psychologist, 46,* 629-639.

Johnson, L. (1994). Cultural competence and sexuality education. In J. Drolet & K. Clark (Eds.), *The sexuality education challenge* (pp. 307-319). Santa Cruz, CA: ETR Associates.

Kaplan, A. (1964). *The conduct of inquiry*. San Francisco: Chandler.

Kinsey, A., Pomeroy, W., & Martin, C. (1948). *Sexual behavior in the human male*. Philadelphia: W.B. Saunders.

Kinsey, A., Pomeroy, W., Martin, C., & Gebhard, P. (1953). *Sexual behavior in the human female*. Philadelphia: W.B. Saunders.

Kirby, D. (1984). *Sexuality education: An evaluation of programs and their effects–An executive summary*. Bethesda, MD: Mathtech, Inc.

Kirkendall, L. (1961). *Premarital intercourse and interpersonal relationships*. New York: Julian.

Kon, I.S. (1988). A sociocultural approach. In J. Geer & W. O'Donohue (Eds.), *Theories of sexuality* (pp. 257-286). New York: Plenum.

Lister, L. (Ed.) (1986). Human sexuality, ethnoculture, and social work. Special Issue of the *Journal of Social Work & Human Sexuality, 4* (3).

Lorand, R. (1965). *Sex and the teenager*. New York: Macmillan.

Maddock, J. (1993). Ecological dialectics: An approach to family theory construction. *Family Science Review, 6,* 137-161.

Maddock, J., & Kon, I.S. (1994). Sexuality and family life. In J. Maddock, M.J. Hogan, A.I. Antonov, & M.S. Matskovsky (Eds.), *Families before and after perestroika* (pp. 96-134). New York: Guilford.

Masters, W., & Johnson, V. (1966). *Human sexual response*. Boston: Little, Brown.

McLuhan, M. (1965). *Understanding media*. New York: McGraw-Hill.

Money, J. (1985). *The destroying angel: Sex, fitness & food in the legacy of degeneracy theory, Graham crackers, Kellogg's corn flakes & American health history*. Buffalo, NY: Prometheus.

Naess, A. (1989). *Ecology, community and lifestyle: Outlines of an ecosophy* (Trans. by D. Rothenberg). Cambridge, England: Cambridge University Press.

Pemberton, L. (1957). *The stork didn't bring you.* New York: Thomas Nelson & Sons.

Reinisch, J., & Beasley, R. (1990). *The Kinsey Institute new report on sex: What you must know to be sexually literate.* New York: St. Martin's Press.

Reiss, I. (1960). *Premarital sexual standards in America: A sociological investigation of the relative social and cultural integration of American sexual standards.* Glencoe, IL: Free Press.

Reiss, I. (1986). *Journey into sexuality: An exploratory voyage.* Englewood Cliffs, NJ: Prentice-Hall.

Reiss, I., & Reiss, H. (1990). *An end to shame: Shaping our next sexual revolution.* Buffalo, NY: Prometheus.

Richardson, H. (1971). *Nun, witch, playmate: The Americanization of sex.* New York: Harper & Row.

Sears, J. (1992). Dilemmas and possibilities of sexuality education: Reproducing the body politic. In J. Sears (Ed.), *Sexuality and the curriculum: The politics and practices of sexuality education* (pp. 7-33). New York: Teachers College Press.

Strong, B. (1972). Ideas of the early sex education movement in America, 1890-1920. *History of Education Quarterly, 12,* 129-161.

WHO Task Force (1975). *Education and treatment in human sexuality: The training of health professionals.* Technical Report No. 572. Geneva, Switzerland: World Health Organization.

Young, W. (1964). *Eros denied: Sex in Western society.* New York: Grove.

Developing Objectives
for an Undergraduate
Human Sexuality Course

Corly J. Petersen, PhD

SUMMARY. The process of developing comprehensive course objectives for an undergraduate course in human sexuality is summarized. The contextual nature of learning, the integrity and coherence of course content, and the role of the educator are discussed. Examples of course content, interactive exercises, communication techniques, and other pedagogical procedures are integrated into the discussion of the rationale for each objective. *[Article copies available for a fee from The Haworth Document Delivery Service: 1-800-342-9678. E-mail address: getinfo@haworth.com]*

Many years ago, a colleague told me of an invaluable human sexuality course she had taken at Syracuse University, taught by a dynamic and charismatic professor, Sol Gordon. Since I did not have the opportunity to take such a course during my time as a student, I was particularly intrigued by her tales of Gordon's ability

---

Corly J. Petersen is affiliated with the Department of Human Development and Family Studies at Iowa State University.

Address correspondence to Corly J. Petersen, Department of Human Development and Family Studies, 101 Child Development Building, Iowa State University, Ames, IA 50011-1030.

[Haworth co-indexing entry note]: "Developing Objectives for an Undergraduate Human Sexuality Course." Petersen, Corly J. Co-published simultaneously in *Journal of Psychology & Human Sexuality* (The Haworth Press, Inc.) Vol. 9, No. 3/4, 1997, pp. 23-35; and: *Sexuality Education in Postsecondary and Professional Training Settings* (ed: James W. Maddock) The Haworth Press, Inc., 1997, pp. 23-35. Single or multiple copies of this article are available for a fee from The Haworth Document Delivery Service [1-800-342-9678, 9:00 a.m. - 5:00 p.m. (EST). E-mail address: getinfo@haworth.com].

23

to present sexually sensitive information in a large lecture hall filled with students. She described how he pulled anonymous questions submitted by students out of a sack and candidly answered them. He employed a respectful sense of humor; but most important, he taught honest and forthright sexuality information, something that most of us were starved for during our undergraduate days.

I had taught at a large midwestern university for 14 years when the opportunity arose for me to teach a course on human sexuality. The course was offered in the College of Family and Consumer Sciences; therefore, I could approach sexuality from a holistic perspective that centered on the family. I was devoted to maintaining scholarly integrity of course content while keeping the students engaged in problem-solving and higher order thinking. I also still carried those images of Sol Gordon's classroom in my mind.

Developing course objectives was the essential first step in designing the course. However, I found the process for devising these objectives distinctly different from other human development courses I had taught. Although sexuality is a universal and integral part of being human, it is a highly sensitive and personal topic. While most students have been exposed to significant amounts of gratuitous and violent sexuality via the media, their sexual knowledge and personal experiences are often cloaked in ignorance and secrecy—yet they are expected to make sexually responsible decisions. In designing sexuality course objectives, it is necessary to be continually aware that the content presented and the learning activities implemented will be filtered through a diverse range of values and moral beliefs, as well as unique personal experiences. Sensitivity to such diversity requires great self-awareness on the part of an instructor, as well as careful consideration of educational objectives.

Course objectives provide direction, parameters, and integrity for course content. Clarity of focus is necessary to provide a coherent curriculum, guided by a vision of the well-educated student (Fitzpatrick, 1994). In a human sexuality course, I prefer to focus on broad educational goals rather than limiting myself to specific behavioral objectives. As proposed by Posner (1991), these broader educational goals can integrate learning across varied personal and educational experiences because they "describe characteristics of the well-educated person" (p. 81). Further, many of these expansive educational concepts are represented in the strategic plans that have been developed by the department, college, and university where I teach. Examples include the ability to solve problems, make informed decisions, think critically, assume social responsibility, understand the diversity that makes each of us unique, and engage in debate on important ideas and issues in which differing opinions are treated with mutual respect (cf., Iowa State University, 1995). I believe that these abilities are crucial to integrate into the objectives for a sexuality course.

Gathering information was an essential first step. While reflecting on my personal desires for outcomes of the course, I found it helpful to review objectives of other sexuality educators and sexuality education programs (DeMauro, 1990; Fishel, 1992; Klein, 1986; Gordon, 1990, 1983; SIECUS, 1991). I also went to the university's student health clinic, as well as to the local offices of the Cooperative Extension Service and Planned Parenthood to obtain materials that might be useful.

Having recognized my desire to formulate course objectives that incorporated these broader educational and societal goals, I found it helpful to organize my thinking into three major conceptual clusters in order to develop and refine the course objectives: *the contextual nature of learning, the coherence of course content, and the pedagogical role of the instructor.*

CONTEXTUAL NATURE OF LEARNING

To better understand the nature of learning, it was necessary to examine the moral, political, legal, and social climates within which learning occurs. As Maddock (1996) points out, the history of sexuality education in North America clearly illustrates the importance and impact of context when developing objectives for a human sexuality course. For example, late in the nineteenth century, the issue of educating women was widely debated. Part of the issue was based upon misinformation about female sexuality. In 1873, a member of the Massachusetts Medical Society and Professor at Harvard College believed that individuals can focus on only one area of personal development at a time, and he warned of the dangers of diverting energy from women when they were in the critical physiological interval for establishing regular menstruation. Edward Clarke (1873) argued that women in such a state who were pressured by the demands of education "graduated from school or college excellent scholars, but with undeveloped ovaries. Later they married, and were sterile" (p. 39). Clarke's formal and stilted discussions of sexual issues represented not only misinformation, but the sentiment of that historical period.

Though we have moved far from the conservative attitudes and lack of knowledge at the turn of the century, continuously changing societal conditions and attitudes still challenge sexuality educators (Friedman, 1992; Gibbs, 1993; Gordon, 1990; Noll, 1995; Sears, 1992; Suggs and Miracle, 1993). New scientific information proliferates while related values are passionately debated. Highly charged political and legal issues such as abortion, sexual orientation, sexual abuse, censorship in cyberspace, and society's response to the HIV/AIDS crisis are debated from moral, religious, legal, cultural, and historical perspectives. In addition, the increasing ethnic and cultural pluralism of U.S. society requires that sexuality education be explicitly cross-cultural, thereby requiring a balance of unity and diversity within a holistic framework.

It is essential that students become knowledgeable about health issues in order to make informed, responsible decisions about their individual sexual behaviors. This responsibility in decision-making extends well beyond themselves to the significant other people in their lives. The vast majority (96%) of the students I teach are 18-24 years of age. Many of them are transitioning from the adolescent phenomena Elkind (1991) describes as the "personal fable." This cognitive self-centeredness convinces an individual that his or her experience is unique and special; as a result, even when facts and consequences of behavior are learned, the individual may fail to apply the knowledge to him/herself. This developmental context is important when designing objectives in sexuality education courses. The personal fables of students challenge sexuality educators to find new ways to substantiate information and to reinforce the consequences of various behaviors.

In order to learn more about the students I am teaching, I administer an 85-item personal profile at the beginning of each term. I have developed this measure from student feedback over the years. Multiple choice questions cover topics such as sexual values, behaviors, preferences, attitudes, self-esteem, sexual attraction, intimacy, honesty, and personal experiences. Student responses are strictly anonymous, classified only by demographic variables such as sex, year in school, ethnicity, marital status, and religion. The survey results provide direct input from the students and assist me in adapting the course objectives for that particular group. For example, students often report communication difficulties in relationships or regrets about some decisions they have made in relation to their sexuality. When this occurs, I place more emphasis on decision-making, problem-solving, and communication skills in the course.

COHERENCE OF COURSE CONTENT

Determining objectives for a coherent and comprehensive human sexuality course in a university setting is a formidable task. Clearly, there is no universal sexuality curriculum (Scales, 1983). Although sexual images and information are ever-present in U.S. society, I find college students eager to learn basic facts about their sexuality and receptive to opportunities to dispel myths. Sexuality educators are continually challenged to select the most relevant, responsible, and current information while adhering to the worthwhile principle of "less is more" (Dempster, 1993). Indeed, it is a challenge to keep abreast of advancing sexuality information. This makes carefully defined course objectives particularly essential as a guide to decisions about content and a framework for organizing course material.

Factual content about sexuality must be combined with skills in personal decision-making and interpersonal communication. As Boyer (1995) points out, courses in colleges and universities need to address the unique contexts of students lives: "Above all, being an educated person means being guided by values and beliefs and connecting the lessons of the classroom to the realities of life" (p. 24). Of course, exactly how students will apply acquired knowledge cannot be known in advance by a course instructor. Offering information and a framework for utilizing the information–including decision-making skills that incorporate values and beliefs–is what the sexuality educator can do. Diversity in both course content and learning activities has the potential for impacting the lives of the greatest number of students in meaningful and useful ways. However, without an interdependent network of realistic course objectives, the overall coherence of a sexuality course is lacking, and information is much less likely to "make sense" to students and, thereby, less likely to be useful in their lives.

PEDAGOGICAL ROLE OF THE INSTRUCTOR

A critical task of an educator is to establish priorities in both course content and learning outcomes. These decisions should be made carefully, based upon a thorough knowledge of potential course content, familiarity with sound theoretical frameworks regarding how students learn, and a commitment to high expectations for learning outcomes. Course objectives that connect the capacities of the learner with both the integrity of course content and the influences of the learning context will be most effective in the educational endeavor. I share with Ayers (1993) the intention to "provoke students from passivity to creative engagement, from indifference to responsible activity, from aimlessness to reflection and wonder at the scope and diversity of a life worth living" (p. 92). It is important to me that the students have opportunities to ask questions, express feelings, clarify values, debate issues, practice communicating, critically evaluate ideas and resources, make decisions, and solve problems. Emphasizing these as learning objectives implies the need for active, cooperative learning experiences. At the same time, by working to implement these objectives, I become a more engaged, interactive educator. And, hopefully, students become more critical, creative thinkers, more likely to continue learning throughout their lives (Boyer, 1990).

Since factual knowledge about sexuality is always embedded within an historical context, educators should strive to provide students with up-to-date, scientifically rigorous information, along with the skills and resources to continue the search for knowledge. By conveying enthusiasm for acquiring knowledge, pointing to reliable sources of information, and demonstrating critical thinking, sexuality educators can model for their students the importance of life-long learning.

AN ILLUSTRATION OF COURSE OBJECTIVES

In university sexuality courses, comprehensive material must be covered using interactive learning methods within significant time constraints. To organize such material, I have developed ten objectives, which provide the coherent framework for the sexuality course I teach. These objectives have been the catalyst for creating interactive experiences, enhancing course content, selecting materials such as readings, and identifying resources such as visiting presenters.

The ten objectives are included in the course syllabus, and I discuss each of them in detail during the first class period. At the end of each semester, I ask the students to reflect on each objective and offer feedback on whether or not the objective was met. I also ask them to judge the personal significance of each objective and to make suggestions for improving the objectives. Thus, the course objectives are continually evolving. Following are the ten course objectives in their current form; I offer them, along with a few comments and illustrations of course design, for consideration.

Objective 1. To optimize the sexual health and well-being of individuals so that they can experience their sexuality in a positive and responsible manner across the life span. Sexuality can be a source of great pleasure, enhancing well-being, or it can be a source of great pain, producing distress and ill health. Many college students report feelings of guilt and shame regarding their sexuality. In the course, I strive to help them understand that their sexuality can become a self-affirming factor in their lives. Enhancing the self-concept is an important prerequisite for establishing mature relationships and promoting sexual responsibility (Francoeur, 1989; Gordon, 1983). My intent is to set a positive tone that reflects the importance of responsibility to self and others, conveying the message that sexuality is an important component of life from the womb to death. This life-span, developmental perspective provides a primary conceptual basis for the course.

Objective 2. To present accurate, factual, comprehensive knowledge of human sexuality. It is important that students understand clearly that the course has a scholarly base; they are held accountable for learning certain facts. Myths are challenged, and misinformation is disputed; reliable information resources are suggested as a basis for informed decision-making. A personalized workbook (Brown, 1994) containing self-study activities corresponds to chapters in the textbook (Byer and Shainberg, 1994). The personal workbook is evaluated three times during the semester, and three objective exams are given.

Objective 3. To strive for understanding of the behavioral, biological, and psychological aspects of human sexuality within the diverse social contexts of family, culture, and society. Bronfenbrenner's (1986, 1993) ecological view of human development provides the basis for understanding sexuality as an interplay of biological, cognitive, and socioemotional processes (Santrock, 1995). Great emphasis is placed upon understanding the impact of the multiple contexts within which the individual operates–family, peer group, neighborhood, community, social policy, and culture–all are important influences. Workbook activities help students reflect upon how they have been socialized and what factors currently influence their decision-making and behavior (though each student has the option to opt out of certain activities for personal reasons).

Objective 4. To keep channels of communication open by requesting and supporting individual efforts to understand and express ideas, feelings, and concerns. Because honest communication is a key to intimate relationships, opportunities are provided for practicing communication skills via such things as the personalized workbook, an anonymous question/comment box in the classroom, and small group activities during the class period. However, personal privacy and safety are also essential; therefore, clear boundaries for class discussions and activities are set by the instructor, both verbally and in writing.

I typically hold office hours immediately after the class meets, since students frequently have a need to process sensitive information that was presented during a session. I have a wide array of referral information readily available.

Objective 5. To develop appreciation for diverse sexual values and lifestyles (with respect for cultural contexts) and to clarify personal sexual values, ethics, and beliefs. Sexuality is typically viewed ethnocentrically. It is important for students to acquire an active appreciation for diversity of all kinds. Comparing and contrasting a wide range of sexual attitudes and behaviors of diverse groups and cultures gives students insight into their own beliefs and practices while developing understanding and tolerance of others (Nevid, Fichner-Rathus, & Rathus, 1995). One of the methods I use to dispel myths and stereotypes is to present the results of the 85-item personal profile completed by students at the beginning of the term. Frequency distributions of female responses, male responses, and combined responses provide an anonymous window into their classmates' attitudes and behaviors. Frequently believing that "everyone" is or is not engaging in a particular behavior, students often are surprised by the results of the survey. Similarly, resource visitors reflecting various sexual lifestyles or life circumstances can have a great impact on students' understanding of diverse sexual attitudes and behaviors. Students are also encouraged to clarify their personal sexual beliefs, values, and preferences in order to better establish clear boundaries. During the final class period, each student develops a "Personal Bill of Sexual Rights."

Objective 6. To increase the ability to evaluate and critically judge validity of sexual research and media representation of sexuality. Materials from both professional and public media, ranging from national publications to local campus materials, can be utilized to encourage critical evaluation of sex-related research, opinion, advertising, and public policy. Ethical research methodology is described and discussed, with particular emphasis on evaluation sources and critique of results. Considerable attention is given to media as a predominant force in contemporary sex education, emphasizing the negative effects of messages that dehumanize and distort sexuality. At the end of the term, students work in small groups to analyze commercial advertisements with regard to social offensiveness and potential impact on various groups of consumers.

Objective 7. To provide opportunities for individuals and small groups to proactively address critical human sexuality issues impacting society. Students are encouraged to view themselves as involved community members and as catalysts for positive change. The course syllabus lists volunteer opportunities available in the community and on the university campus, including such things as a telephone service for crisis intervention, a local sexual assault care center, and a peer health education group. One term, a group of students even developed a successful proposal to install condom vending machines in the residence halls.

Objective 8. To improve communication, problem-solving, and decision-making skills relating to relationships and sexuality issues. Interactive, cooperative-learning experiences offer students opportunities to communicate personally and to problem-solve together, as well as to integrate personal ideas and values with course content. These applied activities need not require preparation outside of class time; they can vary in format and focus on any of the topics of the course, depending upon the interests of the students and my perceptions of issues of importance to each particular class. Given the size of the course (mine is often over 300 students), I have also successfully used a "student representative group" to assist with course planning and feedback. Up to a dozen volunteers meet with me for one hour every other week, to make certain decisions regarding course content, to provide input into course procedures, to offer feedback or problem-solve, and to preview possible films or videos. These informal meetings offer an opportunity for small group interaction and open discussion about the course and the topics.

Objective 9. To assist in locating appropriate and reliable resources for sexuality information. One of my primary goals for sexuality education is to expose students to up-to-date, reliable, easily accessible resources for sexual information. Printed and media resource materials are placed on reserve at the library. Pamphlets and brochures are obtained from the university's student health center and from local health clinics. Toll free numbers and hotline resources are posted among the daily announcements on a large board at the front of the room, and a course homepage on the Internet is currently being developed.

Objective 10. To assist individuals in becoming "askable adults," able to share accurate sexuality information in an age-appropriate manner that is responsive to individual needs and boundaries. Throughout the course, I challenge students to become informal sexuality educators for others–their partners, siblings, friends, or children of their own. Since most students report receiving less sex information from parents than from peers and personal experience, they readily see the need for positive sharing and information dissemination. In a similar way, the importance of respect for boundaries can be recognized and practiced. One successful technique has been to present sexuality education anecdotes for which students can devise hypothetical responses, to be written down and/or discussed in a small group. Such activities help students "rehearse" their responses, providing an opportunity for honest, open communication that can enhance relationships. Hopefully, as adults and parents these students will move beyond "disaster prevention" sex education to ongoing, open, respectful forms of intimacy (Gibbs, 1993).

CONCLUSION

While we face the task of taking teaching methodologies into the 21st century, the effort of designing a comprehensive, coherent, and scholarly sexuality course at the college level remains complex and challenging. One of the most complicated tasks is to devise appropriate sexuality course objectives for an increasingly pluralistic society. Course objectives shape both the structure and process of a sexuality course; therefore, they contribute powerfully to its eventual impact on students. Similarly, course objectives strongly determine the role that the course instructor will play in the educational endeavor. Finally, course objectives reflect the philosophical approach, professional perspective, and even personal values of the instructor.

The process of developing objectives can provide educators with a framework that defines course content and learning activities; however, objectives must continually be adapted to the particular educational setting as well as to the unique characteristics of each group of students. Clearly, all course objectives are interrelated. They reflect their scientific, political, moral, and personal contexts and help convey these influences to the students. By utilizing a process of ongoing assessment and revision of objectives, educators can integrate new developments in the field with emerging needs of students. At their best, course objectives reflect lofty but attainable goals, create a coherent course framework, and encourage scholarly interaction between sexuality educators and their students.

REFERENCES

Ayers, W. (1993). *To teach: The journey of a teacher.* New York: Teachers College Press.

Boyer, E.L. (1990). *Scholarship reconsidered: Priorities of the professoriate.* New Jersey: The Carnegie Foundation for the Advancement of Teaching.

Boyer, E.L. (1995). The educated person. In J. Beane (Ed.), *Toward a coherent curriculum.* Alexandria, VA: Association for Supervision and Curriculum Development.

Bronfenbrenner, U. (1986). Ecology of the family as a context for human development: Research perspectives. *Developmental Psychology, 22,* 723-742.

Bronfenbrenner, U. (1993). Ecological systems theory. In R.K. Wozniak & K. Fischer (Eds.), *Development in context.* Hillsdale, NJ: Erlbaum.

Brown, K.M. (1994). *Student workbook and study guide.* Dubuque, IA: Wm. C. Brown.

Byer, C.O. & Shainberg, L.W. (1994). *Dimensions of human sexuality.* Dubuque, IA: Brown & Benchmark.

Clarke, E.H. (1873). *Sex in education: A fair chance for the girls.* New Hampshire: Ayer Company, Publishers, Inc.

DeMauro, D. (1989-1990, December/January). Sexuality education 1990: A review of state sexuality and AIDS education curricula. *SIECUS Report, 18* (2), 1-9.

Dempster, R. (1993, February). Exposing our students to less should help them learn more. *Phi Delta Kappan, 74,* 432-437.

Elkind, D. (1991). *All grown up and no place to go: Teenagers in crisis.* Reading, MA: Addison-Wesley.

Fishel, E. (1992, September). Raising sexually healthy kids. *Parents,* 110-116.

Fitzpatrick, K.A. (1994). An outcome-based systems perspective on establishing curricular coherence. In J. Beane (Ed.), *Toward a Coherent Curriculum.* Alexandria, VA: Association for Supervision and Curriculum Development.

Francoeur, R.T. (1989). *Taking sides: Clashing views on controversial issues in human sexuality.* Dubuque, IA: Dushkin Publishing Group, Inc.

Friedman, J. (1992, August/September). Cross-cultural perspectives on sexuality education. *SIECUS Report, 20* (6), 5-11.

Gibbs, N. (1993, May). How should we teach our children about sex? *Time,* 60-66.

Gordon, S. (1990, January/February). Sexuality education in the 1990s. *Health Education,* 4-5.

Gordon, S. & Gordon, J. (1983). *Raising a child conservatively in a sexually permissive world.* New York: Simon & Schuster, Inc.

Iowa State University of Science and Technology (1995). *Aspiring to be the nation's premier land-grant university: The strategic plan for 1995-2000.*

Klein, M. (1986). Talking to your kids about sex. *Parents,* 70-74.

Maddock, J.W. (1996). Sexuality education: A history lesson. *Journal of Psychology & Human Sexuality, 9* (3/4), 1-22.

Nevid, J.S., Fichner-Rathus, L. & Rathus, S.A. (1995). *Human sexuality in a world of diversity.* Boston, MA: Allyn & Bacon.

Noll, J.W. (Ed.). (1995). *Taking sides: Clashing views on controversial educational issues.* Connecticut: Dushkin.

Posner, G.J. (1992). *Analyzing the Curriculum.* New York: McGraw-Hill, Inc.

Santrock, J.W. (1995). *Life-span development.* Dubuque, IA: Brown & Benchmark.

Scales, P. (1983, April). Today's sexuality education represents the essence of democratic society. *Family Relations,* 109-118.

Sears, J.T. (Ed.). (1992). *Sexuality and the Curriculum.* New York: Teachers College Press.

SIECUS National Guidelines Task Force. (1991). *Guidelines for comprehensive sexuality education.* New York: Author.

Suggs, D.N. & Miracle, A.W. (Eds.). (1993). *Culture and human sexuality.* California: Brooks/Cole.

Celebrating Diversity:
Feminist Sexuality Education
in the Undergraduate Classroom

Naomi B. McCormick, PhD

SUMMARY. Questioning the validity of the middle-class, white, male, heterosexual standard of sexual normality, feminist sexuality education celebrates diversity by considering how socioeconomic class, ethnicity, race, religion, region, gender, sexual orientation, age, and physical health or disability function independently and in interaction to shape sexual attitudes and experience. Students are treated as active participants in the learning process, not passive vessels to be filled up with facts. Instruction focuses on affective and cognitive learning simultaneously. This article considers a variety of techniques for empowering students to share thoughts and feelings both in the classroom and through individual and collective homework assignments. By treating those we teach as colleagues, not subordinates, and by attending to individual growth and group process, teachers become students too, taking emotional risks in the classroom, opening ourselves to new information, and being willing to listen to students' criticism and suggestions for improvement. *[Article copies available for a fee from The Haworth Document Delivery Service: 1-800-342-9678. E-mail address: getinfo@haworth.com]*

Naomi B. McCormick is affiliated with the Department of Design & Family Consumer Science, University of Northern Iowa.

Address correspondence to Naomi B. McCormick, Department of Design & Family Consumer Science, University of Northern Iowa, Cedar Falls, IA 50614-0332.

[Haworth co-indexing entry note]: "Celebrating Diversity: Feminist Sexuality Education in the Undergraduate Classroom." McCormick, Naomi B. Co-published simultaneously in *Journal of Psychology & Human Sexuality* (The Haworth Press, Inc.) Vol. 9, No. 3/4, 1997, pp. 37-69; and: *Sexuality Education in Postsecondary and Professional Training Settings* (ed: James W. Maddock) The Haworth Press, Inc., 1997, pp. 37-69. Single or multiple copies of this article are available for a fee from The Haworth Document Delivery Service [1-800-342-9678, 9:00 a.m. - 5:00 p.m. (EST). E-mail address: getinfo@haworth.com].

37

Not long ago, Bonnie Nelson Trudell (1993) published an insightful ethnography describing a ninth-grade sexuality education class taught in a predominantly white, American public high school located in a conservative, middle-class, midwestern community. The teacher, Trudell observed, instructed students to adhere to traditional, European-American sex roles and heterosexual values by making use of:

> "defensive teaching" strategies–selecting mostly noncontroversial topics, limiting substantive student discussion, presenting easily transmitted and graded fragments of technical details . . . These [pedagogic strategies] had the effect of reducing the complex and value-laden topic of sexuality to simplified and irrelevant school knowledge. (Trudell, 1993, p. 97)

Nonetheless, students were not always silenced. Instead, Trudell pointed out, the young high school students–especially those who felt marginalized in the predominantly white, middle-class school used "informal bantering" to challenge the teacher's conservative sexual discourse (p. 8).

According to Trudell, African-American students and "dirts" (young, sexually rebellious, white girls from working class families) used banter to question the conservative sexuality education they received. One girl, for example, responded to the teacher's statement that abstinence is completely risk-free and "100 percent effective in preventing pregnancy" by quipping that an individual who abstained from sexual intercourse could get "herpes by mouth" or "turn out to be a cranky librarian" (p. 99).

Like all too many classroom teachers, the ninth grade health educator studied by Trudell (1993) taught about sexuality as if it took place in a social and political vacuum. The diversity of sexual experience and values among individuals varying in sexual orientation, ethnicity, social class, and health status were never examined.

> Students were offered a perception of heterosexual intercourse as the most legitimate expression of sexuality–particularly in the context of reproduction, and parenting among mature and financially secure adults. . . . Other forms of sexual expression such as homosexual activity, masturbation, and oral sex were

mentioned only in connection with gay males, and the consequences of AIDS. (p. 129)

In contrast with actual practice, the majority of ninth-grade sex
education students interviewed by Trudell (1993) wanted to learn
more about sexual diversity and homosexuality in particular. Affirming information about lesbian, gay, and bisexual persons and
alternative sex roles might have circumvented the relentless and
cruel teasing about being "fags" directed at some students. Unfortunately, the undercurrent of antigay and sexist "humor" in the
classroom was generally ignored by the teacher.

Other than linking homosexuality to AIDS and attempting to
treat her African-American students fairly, the teacher studied by
Trudell remained silent on such issues of sexual diversity as gay and
lesbian life, homohatred, disability, sexism, racism, and class prejudice. Sexual information was presented "largely as fact or detail,
receiving no elaboration beyond a few sentences" in a seemingly
random order (p. 107). Much of class time was spent having students listen to the teacher "read pieces of information aloud" which
they recorded on worksheets for later study (p. 108). Course content
as well as teacher interactions presented human sexuality as a potentially dangerous activity best limited to marriage with traditional
sex roles and white, able-bodied, middle-class standards for sexual
behavior depicted as normative for all of humanity.

As Janice Irvine (1995) points out:

> Our ideas about sexuality—what it is and where it comes from—
> are critically important to sexuality education. That is because
> how we think about sexuality shapes how we talk about it. . . .
> Even if we are not consciously aware of our assumptions
> about sexuality, they exert a tremendous influence. (p. 1)

Like Irvine and Trudell, I believe that many sexuality education
classes ignore diversity and the female experience, falsely present-
ing students with a homogenous, male model of what it means to be
sexual. Like their counterparts in middle and secondary schools,
undergraduate sexuality educators all too often regard the sexual
scripts of dominant groups as essentialist truths, enduring across
time and cultures. Describing a feminist alternative to conventional

sexuality education, this article draws upon my nearly two decades of experience teaching undergraduates about human sexuality. In addition to criticizing conventional pedagogy, I will describe a variety of techniques and resources for helping students understand and celebrate sexual diversity.

FEMINIST PERSPECTIVES

Traditional sexuality education and research assumes a male, heterosexual, white, middle-class, able-bodied, young adult standard of "normal" sexuality (Babb, 1994; Irvine, 1995; McCormick, 1994a; Tiefer, 1987, 1988, 1995; Yoder & Kahn, 1993). Like other feminist educators, I propose instead a sexual science of diversity that includes the perspectives of women, gay, lesbian, and bisexual people and people of color. A sexual science of diversity would also consider the perspectives of poor and working-class individuals, not just those from the middle class. Of course, feminist sexuality education would provide affirming information on persons who live with disabilities and chronic illness. Here too, ageism would be challenged, and students would learn about the sexual attitudes and experiences of diverse women and men of all ages.

Rather than looking at group membership simplistically, the feminist sexuality educator notes that individuals belong to multiple groups, each of which influences sexual experiences like a thread running through their lives (Fine, 1992; Maher & Tetreault, 1994). For example, if we want to understand a particular woman's sexuality, we need to frame it in terms of all her identities. The sexual values and experiences of a middle-aged lesbian who is African-American and employed as a professional are bound to differ from that of a younger lesbian of color, a working-class African-American lesbian, and a heterosexual woman from the same ethnic group. Students need to know that there is no such thing as the average woman or man, the average gay person, the average person of color, or the average physically disabled person.

The feminist sexuality educator helps students dispute prejudice while increasing both self-acceptance and tolerance of others. Feminist sexuality education prepares students for living and loving in a constantly changing world. Instructors who practice inclusive, feminist sexuality education refuse to limit information about nondominant groups to a textbook or curriculum "ghetto," considered only as special cases during limited times in the semester (Fine, 1992; Maher & Tetreault, 1994; McCormick, 1994a). Gay, lesbian, and bisexual persons and physically disabled persons are discussed throughout the course, not just when students read a "special chapter" about sexual orientation or "disability." People of color, disabled persons, and individuals of all ages would be considered in every segment of the course, not just when "social problems" like early sexual activity, adolescent pregnancy, teenage motherhood, AIDS and other sexually transmitted diseases, and sexual problems associated with disability and aging are addressed.

The typical college sexuality textbook–indeed the typical undergraduate course–treats human sexual development as a uniform process. White, young, able-bodied, middle-class heterosexuals are the normative group. In the typical college sexuality text, most of the research cited is limited to studies of this socially privileged group. An inclusive, feminist course would provide students with additional information. Students would read about and discuss the sexual development of working-class and poor people, of individuals from various ethnic groups and cultures, of the physically disabled or chronically ill, and of course–of individuals who grow up to be and live most or all of their adult lives as lesbian, gay, or bisexual persons. To achieve this goal, instructors could ask students to read biographical and autobiographical narratives as well as novels, short stories, and poetry, telling in their own words, the stories of diverse women and men.

Given the paucity of culturally sensitive sex research, empirical information alone may not be sufficient for those who wish to design an inclusive course (Irvine, 1995). In Appendix A, I provide readers with an "Annotated Bibliography of Resources for Feminist Teachers and Selected Biographical or Literary Materials Useful for Feminist Sexuality Education." Of course, readers will want to update my list, exploring the increasing number of excellent narrative publications by feminist, minority, lesbian-gay-bisexual, and disabilities rights scholars.

Appendix B, "Internet Resources for Feminist Sexuality Education," indicates a select number of the prolific electronic and Internet resources available to sexuality instructors who have access to computers. These resources not only yield ideas for possible reading assignments but also give feminist instructors an opportunity to exchange teaching ideas with like-minded scholars and teachers all over the world.

Inclusive, feminist pedagogy encourages students to ask and discuss important questions that would be ignored in a conventional course, for example: How might adolescence be experienced by a mobility-impaired individual? What are long-term relationships like when one or both partners has a serious physical disability? What might sexual expression be like for disabled gay men and lesbians? Students should consider, not only access to birth control and abortion, but also gay and lesbian parenting and the reproductive rights and desires of physically disabled persons. Classroom discussion of sexual pleasure should consider the experiences of individuals varying in sexual orientation and age. Included also should be information about the influence of pain, chronic illness, physical disability, and medication on sexual self-image, pleasure, and intimacy.[1]

Feminist sexuality education and research take a critical stance towards conventional social science descriptions of the association between group membership and sexual behaviors and attitudes (McCormick, 1994a; Samuels, 1993; Wyatt, 1994). Just because individuals belong to a particular group does not necessarily imply that their sexual behavior or experiences are caused by group membership. When comparing African-Americans' and white European Americans' contraceptive practices and experiences with sexually transmitted disease and abortion, I always remind students that social class differences often wash out ethnic differences. In other words, many of the so-called differences between white persons and persons of color are best accounted for by socioeconomic status. When income is controlled (all research participants are middle-class and highly educated), numerous so-called racial or ethnic differences evaporate.

Feminist sexuality education helps students factor in individual differences in sexual experience and recognize that sexual scientists are not immune from prejudice. Students should be informed, not just about good sex research, but also about reprehensible research.

As a case in point, in *Sexuality education across cultures,* Janice Irvine (1995) discusses the Tuskegee Syphilis Study conducted by the U.S. Public Health Service from 1932 until 1972. Six-hundred African-American men were recruited to assess the effects of untreated syphilis and determine if race was a factor in the developmental course of the disease. Racism shaped this study from the inception; the scientists never questioned their assumption that African-Americans were inferior and promiscuous. Deceived, participants were told neither their diagnosis nor the true purpose of the research. The scientists did nothing to help the men or their loved ones even though it was in their power to do so.

> When penicillin . . . became the standard treatment in 1951, it was withheld from the subjects. Researchers made the decision to allow the disease to spread, unchecked, until the men died . . . and could be examined in an autopsy. (Irvine, 1995, p. 49)

Laud Humphreys' (1975) *Tearoom trade* provides students with another example of ethically troublesome research linked, not to racism, but to a violation of the privacy of men whom Humphreys observed engaging in impersonal homosexual activity in public toilets (or "tearooms") located in urban parks. Posing as a sympathetic lookout, Humphreys secretly recorded the license plate numbers of automobiles parked outside the tearooms where men engaged in impersonal sex. Disguising the fact that he had observed these men having sex with strangers, Humphreys interviewed his subjects one year later in their own homes for a supposed community health survey. Humphreys justified his methodology by noting that he had learned something very important. Despite their apparently "deviant" sexual behavior, the majority of men he had observed presented themselves as happily married, pillars of the community. To his credit, Humphreys safeguarded the identities of the men he studied from police and other authorities. However, those he watched and later interviewed had never given him their informed consent.

Humphreys' decision to track down the true identities of men that he had observed engaging in illegal homosexual activity in public toilets stimulates a great deal of discussion in my classes.

Generally, students wonder aloud if individuals who engaged in clandestine and illegal heterosexual activities would have been subjected to the same risky, intrusive, and deceptive assessment procedures as Humphreys' subjects faced for engaging in "deviant" homosexual activity. My students and I seriously doubt that the answer to this question would be "yes." Humphreys' methodological decisions suggest wrongfully that the scientist has an inalienable right to be a voyeur, especially if the people he or she investigates are members of a sexual minority. Students benefit immensely from a consideration of the implications of sexual science for human rights and tolerance.

After asking students to read original research, we can stimulate their critical thinking skills by encouraging them to consider a number of important issues. How might racism affect sex research on black teenagers? Why is most of the research on this group concerned with "sexual problems," such as adolescent pregnancy and risk for sexually transmitted disease? Alternatively, how might homohatred shape research on the etiology of sexual orientation or sexual risk-taking? Why are scientists so obsessed with "problematic" aspects of being a gay man or lesbian while mainstream sexual pleasure literature ignores the joys of gay and lesbian sexuality? How and why might ageism and prejudice against the disabled inspire studies and clinical descriptions which depict the elderly and disabled as asexual persons who enjoy a "lesser sexuality" than the young and able-bodied? Why does the typical textbook describe the sexualities of disabled or elderly persons solely in chapters on failing health or sexual "dysfunctions"? Shouldn't information about these groups be mainstreamed throughout the text in chapters on sexual pleasure and "normal" human development?

Fortunately, students are often feminist educators' best allies. As the undergraduate student body becomes more diverse, with increasing numbers of women, members of sexual and cultural minority groups, older students, and students with disabilities, these students become educational resources for their classmates and instructors (Thompson, 1993). In my own classes, students from nondominant groups help classmates overcome prejudices and negative stereotypes and assist me in correcting misinformation conveyed by required readings.

Ultimately, feminism inspires sexuality educators to consider the limits of traditional science in capturing or understanding human sexuality (Riger, 1992). Sexual science reflects, not only the values of individual researchers, but also the larger political and cultural climate. When discussing research on sexual orientation, for instance, it is valuable to ask students why the scientists primarily investigate why people become homosexual, seldom inquiring about the reasons for heterosexuality. In her interactive college textbook, *Exploring our sexuality,* Patricia Barthalow Koch (1995) invites students to contemplate this issue by asking the unexpected: "What is heterosexuality? How do you know if someone is hetero-sexual? What percentage of people in our country are heterosexual? What causes heterosexuality?. . . . Since there is such a high rate of divorce . . ., why is it so difficult for heterosexuals to stay in committed relationships?. . . . Can heterosexuality be changed or cured? How?" (pp. 123-128). Helping students grasp the impor-tance of this exercise, Koch (1995) writes:

> The preceding questions are commonly asked, not about het-erosexuality, but about homosexuality. It is not unusual for gay men and lesbian women to be asked these questions by people they hardly know, as well as their friends and family . . . what can be silly, insensitive, or insulting about such questions is that they are usually limited to homosexuality instead of being applied to the entire range of sexual orientation, including exclusive heterosexuality. (p. 129)

By reading and discussing published sexuality research, students can familiarize themselves with the methodological and philosophi-cal limitations of sexual science. For example, critical thinking can be stimulated by asking students whether scientists who study the supposed prevalence of homosexuality are missing something by operationally defining sexual orientation as an individual's genital activities during the previous year.

A critical feminist stance in sexuality education would inspire students to examine the possibility that knowledge is not neutral, but serves an ideological purpose. Early in the semester, it is worth-while to ask students why most funded "respectable" sexuality research focuses on "sexual problems" as defined by conservative, middle-class, heterosexual adults–adolescent sexual activity, sexually transmitted disease, teenage pregnancy, sexual abuse and violence, the "causes" of homosexuality, commercial sex and pornography and the like. Research on sexual pleasure, affirming information on the sexual expression of nondominant groups, and girls/women as independent sexual actors (not victims) is rarely funded or taken seriously (Fine, 1992; Irvine, 1995; McCormick, 1994a).

We can teach students that feminist and humanistic sexual science is based on collaboration (that is doing something *with* research participants rather than doing something *to* them). Here are some undergraduates describing feminist science (McCormick, in press):

> When I [first] heard the word research, I would envision men in white coats walking down a gloomy hallway to find deep, dark hidden secrets. . . . [Now] I think that research should produce more knowledgeable action in the world, not just more knowledge of the problem.
>
> I have learned that feminist research must first and foremost incorporate the voices of the participants.
>
> It is vital to give something back to society by doing research. Ideally feminists try to establish a give and take relationship with those that they are getting information from. . . . This sort of give and take relationship resembles . . . friendship whereas in mainstream research, the research-subject relationship is much more hierarchical.

Ultimately, feminist sexual science and sexuality education are concerned with accountability. Instead of stripping out social context, the feminist sexuality educator celebrates sociocultural and historical factors that help shape sexual behavior and attitudes (Maher & Tetreault, 1994).

Instead of viewing the sexuality educator as ultimate authority, students in the feminist classroom are asked to be verbally expressive and reflective (Maher & Tetreault, 1994). Students may conduct small observational studies and share the results in papers and group discussion. At various times, I have asked students to observe similarities and differences between women and men flirting in bars or at parties, describe how they felt and how others reacted when they purchased condoms at a retail outlet, and analyze the messages about love and intimacy provided by popular songs and films, framing all of this in terms of required readings and scientific findings. I have also found it helpful to give traditional assignments such as asking students to critically analyze published research in sexual science, framing their discussion in terms of methodological and conceptual problems that consider gender and human inclusivity. When discussing this scientific work in class, it is important for teachers like myself to listen to all viewpoints with respect and to emphasize a diversity of plausible interpretations.

FEMINIST PEDAGOGY

Feminist sexuality education should do more than provide students with inclusive information about the sexualities of diverse groups and should be more than a post-modern critique of conventional science. Feminist sexuality education begins with a vision of what the classroom might be but usually isn't, a liberatory environment in which teachers and students are equally active and responsible for instruction and learning (Shrewsbury, 1993).

The feminist educator pays close attention to spontaneous remarks and group processes. Discussion is guided at least partially by students' questions and observations (Maher & Tetreault, 1994). Students, especially minority and women students, are encouraged to find their own sexual voices. As described earlier and illustrated in Appendixes A and B, this goal is often best achieved by supplementing traditional texts and audiovisual materials with discussion of readings and films on individuals who differ from dominant groups in age, socioeconomic class, ethnicity or race, religion, disability status, and/or sexual orientation.

An inclusive sexuality class is not just emotionally powerful, it is a rich intellectual experience. Whenever I ask students to read autobiographical, biographical, or literary narratives about someone's sexual and life experiences, I also require them to use scientific research and theory to frame their analyses. For example, I recommend Beverly Donofrio's book (1990), *Riding in cars with boys:*

Confessions of a bad girl who makes good in Appendix A of this article. For a number of years, students have responded well to this assignment:

> After reading *Riding in cars with boys*, summarize how Beverly Donofrio describes her life . . . Keep this summary as brief and factual as possible; the rest of your paper will be interpretative. Next, analyze the way that Beverly Donofrio's life was developmentally and socially constructed. *For this interpretative part of your paper, make sure that you answer at least two of these three questions*: (1) How would a *developmental psychologist* explain Donofrio's sexual and social behavior? Discuss maturational issues. (2) How would a *feminist sexologist* explain Donofrio's life. Describe how sex-role socialization, and prevailing attitudes towards girls and women shaped her experiences and insights in both positive and negative ways. Note here the extent to which Donofrio's feelings about herself and sexual experiences were shaped by the cultural expectation that all women should be heterosexual. How would her life have been different had she experimented with bisexuality or came out as a lesbian at some point? (3) How would a *sociologist* explain Donofrio's sexual and social behavior? Take into consideration demographic variables which are important such as her family's socioeconomic status (social class), ethnicity and race, the nature of the community in which she grew up, deviant subcultures she identified with, economic issues faced by pregnant teenagers with limited education, and the historical context of her life. (McCormick, 1994b)

Students' knowledge of sexual diversity and critical thinking skills can be stimulated in a variety of ways. Here is a similar assignment, applied this time to another reference listed in Appendix A, *Women on women: An anthology of American lesbian short fiction* (Nestle & Holoch, 1990).

> After reading all of the assigned stories in *Women on women,* pick between three and six stories to write about. In this assignment, you will be doing a dialogue with the text,

having a conversation with the story's author and your professor about what you strongly liked or disliked and why. Most students will find it helpful to prepare a separate dialogue for each story, each numbered sequentially. Here are some suggestions on strategy.

First, write the number and title of the story. Next, pick a *brief* passage or quote from the story that made you think or generated a strong emotional reaction. . . . Make sure that you indicate the page numbers of any direct quotes. Now, express your own feelings or opinions. These can take any or all of the following forms:

Challenges or Criticisms–Examples: What does the author mean by . . .? The author doesn't say enough about . . . I disagree with the author's point of view because . . . This gives an incorrect impression of . . . because . . . I was really upset by this because . . . This is really a disservice to the goals of activists in the Gay Lesbian Rights movement because . . .

Affirmations–Examples: I agree with this idea because . . . I liked or sympathized with characters in this story because . . . This appeals to me because I have had similar experiences such as . . . I know what the author is talking about because . . . This reminds me of . . . This really tickled my sense of humor because . . . I was deeply moved by this since . . .

Questions–Examples: This really puzzles me because . . . I think that the typical reader would be confused by this because . . . This doesn't make any sense for the following reasons . . . I am lost because this contradicts what we learned in class in the following ways . . .

Finally, write a paragraph or two that ties the story you read to information from . . . [this sexuality class] and perhaps other Women's Studies and Psychology courses. What, if anything, might the story add or fail to add to sexual scientists' understanding of sex roles or lesbian sexuality? Remember, the tighter your scholarship (the more skilled you are in integrating the fictional story with academic knowledge, especially fully cited material), the higher your grade will be. (McCormick, 1993)

Some instructors may be interested in helping students better appreciate the multiplicity of sexual experiences across the lifespan. With this goal in mind, I have asked students in their late teens and early twenties to collect and analyze scientific articles on middle aged and older persons who vary in socioeconomic status, sexual orientation, health, and ethnicity. After reading several recent articles, students are asked to write essays indicating what they have learned from the readings and how they anticipate this information will be relevant to their own lives (McCormick, 1995a). Generally, the assignment helps students feel less anxious about aging and develop more empathy for older persons, including their parents and instructor!

In the feminist classroom, students' insights are not just reserved for the instructor's eyes. For all assignments described above, I ask students to discuss and share what they have learned in small groups and with the class as a whole.

Feminist sexuality education emphasizes active learning. In courses enrolling up to 100 students (the smaller, the better), it is possible to structure class time so that it is assumed that students do the reading and prepare daily homework assignments to talk about in class. Straight lectures are inconsistent with feminist pedagogy. Teachers should not be the only ones prepared for class! By grading students partially on their class preparation and contributions to discussion, by employing various group discussion and even "talk show" techniques, it is possible for the classroom of thirty to sixty students to take on the character of a seminar (or so my students tell me).

Here are some exercises I have used to stimulate group discussion and critical thinking in college sexuality classes. Early in the semester, I may ask students to write down "What is sex or having sex?" I follow this with a feminist discourse analysis of traditional androcentric views of sexuality and sex therapy in our field. In my analysis, I make sure to differentiate between anonymous student essays that describe sex in terms of physiological activities (the sexual response cycle) and those which focus on intimacy and communication, being careful to praise the wisdom of both views while fostering group discussion. In one such class, students spontaneously noted that some men in our college community refer to having sex as "closing the deal." The group had fun discussing the implications of this sexual terminology and how and why it was not dissimilar from the orgasm-as-goal ideology perpetuated by conventional sexual science.

Another valuable classroom activity is to ask students to prepare voluntary, anonymous, in-class, brief descriptions of their "worst experiences with sexual exploitation or coercion," defined in their own words. Before the next class, I complete a content or discourse analysis of these descriptions and use this information to help students appreciate the research (including statistical information) on the prevalence of sexual aggression that they are exposed to in formal reading assignments. If handled with sensitivity, this type of assignment helps students who have had negative experiences with sexual coercion feel validated while stimulating greater consciousness regarding sexual violence and increased empathy for victims among students as a whole. A segment from a handout provided to students after the class completed such an exercise, and used to stimulate further discussion, follows:

> Eighty-one percent [who elected to complete this in-class assignment] described being survivors of one or more forms of sexual coercion. The results were similar to a survey completed by students in this class during previous semesters . . . Nearly half the students (48%) who completed questionnaires described having survived an attempted or completed acquaintance rape . . . Another 9 percent of the sample [indicated that they had experienced some form of] . . . childhood [or adolescent] sexual abuse. . . . Almost all (94%) of the self-described victims were women. . . . [For example, one woman wrote: "I was at a fraternity party when a brother . . . asked me if I wanted to go on a tour of the house. He led me right to his bedroom . . . I was buzzing really bad. He went to his closet where he got a condom. Immediately, I jumped up and told him that he had the wrong idea. He said he didn't and pushed me on his bed. I fought him as he undid my belt. We struggled and he held my arms down and put his knees on my arms. . . . He unzipped his pants and . . . glared. . . . [when I struggled] . . . I was scared." (McCormick, 1992)

If fortunate, educators can inspire students to transform what they learn in classroom into feminist action or research. In my smaller feminist, sexuality classes (enrolling 15 to 25 individuals), students complete a reading log or reaction journal, described in greater detail later. This reaction journal asks students to describe a feminist research idea or positive social action idea, if any, that was inspired by the daily, required reading assignment. Sometimes, these ideas develop into major academic projects. For example, a reading assignment on prostitution inspired a student who majored in Communication as well as Psychology to complete a discourse analysis of how female sex workers are portrayed in film, television, and popular magazines. A second student in this same course was inspired by a book on courtship and popular culture to complete a content analysis in which she and an independent rater compared the sex role and sexuality messages presented in women's magazines marketed mainly to the following groups: adolescents, older women, and African-American women. In another class, a young man was inspired by his readings on sexuality and disability to initiate a project that examined the insights into health care and sexual self-image shared in women's published breast cancer narratives. In a different class still, a reading assignment on rape inspired a student who had worked with rape victims as a paramedic and ambulance driver to write a paper integrating her applied experience with the scientific and feminist literature. All four of these students ended up reporting their research at regional scientific meetings and a campus "showcase" program for undergraduate scholarship; two of these research projects were actually funded (McCormick, Leonard, Santor, Moore, & Ibanez, 1993; McCormick, 1995b).

Ideally, the feminist sexuality educator works with a small, enthusiastic, diverse, academically well-prepared group of students in an institution that supports quality teaching (Maher & Tetreault, 1994). This occurs most often at selective liberal arts colleges which are unabashedly devoted to teaching. At Spelman College, founded to educate black women in 1881, multicultural feminist pedagogy is celebrated with the goal of creating bridges between African-American students and black (including poor) communities. Sometimes, larger universities with a lower faculty to student ratio also emphasize feminist, multicultural teaching. For example,

San Francisco State University is noted for having a highly ethnically diverse and class-conscious student body and a proud and visible lesbian and gay student presence (Maher & Tetreault, 1994). This kind of student diversity can be a great asset to the feminist sexuality educator.

Unfortunately, teaching environments do not always welcome feminist approaches or even sexuality education per se. Feminist sexuality education practice must be modified depending on the teacher's status and power within an institution, college resources, and work demands made on instructors.

In their ethnographic study of feminist college teachers, some of whom taught human sexuality, Maher and Tetrault (1994) learned that those employed in major, large, research and grant-oriented universities were least innovative in their pedagogy, in part because of large class size and competing institutional demands. In such institutions, good teaching was equated with consciously, rational discourse. Inconsistent with feminist instructional goals, professors perceived themselves as the ultimate experts in the discipline, with duty to impart knowledge (top-down) to students (who were regarded as passive learners). In this type of institution, feminist instructors may wish to experiment with a variety of active-learning techniques designed for larger classes.

Sexuality instructors who teach 50 to 150 students may want to experiment with Socratic and peer-mentored pedagogy. In the Socratic classroom, instructors call upon students to answer questions and make comments about daily reading assignments, simultaneously encouraging students to engage one another in discussion and debate. Peer-mentored instructors hand out discussion questions to small groups facilitated by undergraduate teaching assistants. Eventually, group members share insights with the class as a whole. Nametags help instructors learn each student's name and designate credit for class participation. Daily homework assignments and unannounced, open-notes quizzes are supplementary tools for positively reinforcing class preparation.

Despite the academic rigor of active-learning approaches, focus group data suggests that students who receive this type of instruction are more likely to describe a warm classroom environment than those who are taught through lectures. These student comments from my focus group research clarify that an empathic Socratic instructor can make a large class feel like a warm, learning community (McCormick & Burke, 1996):

> I think it's different in the sense that–for me–we feel more comfortable. Like, if I go into a class where there's just a lecture . . . I'm just one of the crowd. [Here], I feel more comfortable. I can ask questions and I talk more than I've ever done before in class. And I can interact with other people and their opinions and stuff like that. So, it makes it more fun being in a class and not just sit[ting] there look[ing] at the time.
>
> The thing that I like about her approach is that you can talk to her without feeling ridiculous or anything. . . . At the beginning, I was very afraid . . . you know. She made me feel like I could do it, like I was smart.

Here is how students described a popular teacher's peer-mentored instructional method in my focus group research (McCormick & Burke, 1996).

> I think the most important thing is that she respects all of us and then we respect each other. I think she's almost more of another student, kind of, than a teacher. We all talk to each other, so we're all students together at the same time.
>
> I like how she involves or tries to involve everybody to participate in speaking in class, she always backs everybody's opinion, she really doesn't put anybody's opinion down; she always incorporates it in what she is speaking about.

Like it or not, the academic culture for campus feminists is likely to mirror that of the college or university as a whole. If publications and grants are emphasized at the expense of teaching, class size may become too large for meaningful intellectual interactions. Students in turn are likely to feel anonymous and silenced, no matter how "feminist" their reading assignments or instructors might be. Yes, creative feminist pedagogy can be employed in larger classes, but feminist sexuality education is probably impossible when classes number greater than 200.

Maher and Tetreault (1994) have also studied feminist teachers at medium selective, public, nondoctoral, coed universities (similar to my own school). Here, faculty have lower status, a worse budget, and greater teaching demands than at major universities and elite colleges. At the same time, faculty are given confusing and mixed messages about their roles. Teaching is supposedly highly valued, but promotions and praise may be more contingent upon faculty research and grant activity. Quality teaching is also hindered by increasing class size and numbers of required instructor preparations as administrators respond to the squeeze of fiscally conservative governors and state legislatures. Here too, students may regard college, not so much as a learning community, but as a place for vocational training in the service of upward mobility. Facing these institutional pressures, feminist teaching may become devalued or marginalized. Given institutional dynamics such as this, the individual who wishes to teach a feminist sexuality class may be obliged to either give up this desire or teach a course overload, neither prospect of which is likely to be welcomed. Alternatively, the instructor is faced with the task of selling the intellectual and emotional benefits of "feminist" pedagogy to students who are largely vocationally-oriented.

Pessimism about the academy aside, there are a number of useful writing assignments available to instructors interested in fostering both active-learning and feminist sexuality education. Especially useful are journals in which students' ongoing reactions to readings and class process are shared. Literature teachers and others in the humanities call this type of assignment a "dialogue"; feminist psychologist Michael Stevenson calls it a "reaction journal" (Gussman & Hesford, 1992; Stevenson, 1989). I ask students in classes of up to 30 individuals to have their dialogue or reaction journal on the daily reading assignment available for their use at the beginning of class. This is a jumping off point for intellectual discussion and meaningful emotional sharing. Students are free to add additional comments, inspired by group discussion, to their dialogue or journal assignments before handing them in at the end of class. I have reproduced two such reaction journals in Table 1. When provided to students, of course, I allow ample space for their written comments and insights.

TABLE 1. Sample Reaction Journals for Feminist Sexuality Classes

---

Reaction Journal for Small Class or Seminar

[ ]   QUESTIONS
[ ]   PERSONAL GOALS FOR TODAY'S CLASS
[ ]   WHAT I LIKED ABOUT READINGS AND/OR CLASS DISCUSSION
[ ]   WHAT I DISLIKED ABOUT READINGS AND/OR CLASS DISCUSSION
[ ]   INSIGHTS FROM TODAY'S ASSIGNMENT AND/OR DISCUSSION
[ ]   OTHER COMMENTS

Daily Written Assignment for Larger Class

I. Write one or two question(s) you had about the assigned reading.
II. Write down the *most important thing you learned* from reading this chapter (*maximum of two or three sentences*). State your insight in your own words. If possible, relate what you have learned to an experience or observance from your own life including material covered in another class.

Reaction journals can serve multiple educational purposes. First, they may be a nonthreatening way to see that students have completed required readings. Second, instructors can facilitate class discussion by asking students to refer to their reaction journals for questions they may have about the readings or comments on material that they liked or disliked. Students in my classes generally delight in being able to criticize required readings and often report that mine has been the first class structured to welcome their criticism of the so-called experts in the field.

It is imperative that teachers read and respond in writing to students' comments in reaction journals. Often, this is a way for the teacher to keep her or his finger on the emotional pulse of classroom. In reaction journals, if not in the class as a whole, students may voice negative feelings about course content, the teacher, other students, and themselves which can be addressed appropriately in the future. By responding warmly and sensitively to students' comments, we can reassure them that all opinions and experiences are welcomed, not just those of the instructor or majority of students. Reaction journals help feminist sexuality teachers forge a learning community (or as my students say, a caring family within the academy where their opinions and confidentiality will be safeguarded).

Reaction journals do more than contribute to a warm emotional climate in the classroom. They provide feminist teachers with additional opportunities to respond personally to each student and address commonly held misconceptions. For example, students often respond to course content on homosexuality or erotica with "knee-jerk" religious arguments about how and why homosexuality or pornography is sinful or wrong. In their comments on such journals, instructors can show respect for students' religious and moral convictions while referring them to appropriate scholarly or scientific resources on sexual orientation and/or erotica.

Reaction journals can help instructors make the classroom more egalitarian while helping students work through problematic aspects of group process. Some students express anger or disappointment in the instructor in their journals; others write about their misgivings of other students. Without identifying the writer, instructors can use this information to help the class as a whole, praising the group for their constructive criticism and inviting members to voice their concerns aloud in future class meetings.

Process comments in students' reaction journals are especially helpful when course content touches upon individuals' personal experiences. Many students struggle with their emerging identity as lesbians, gay men, or bisexual persons in a homohating campus and culture. All too many have experienced racism, sexual coercion or abuse, and even domestic violence in close relationships. Although the classroom should never be a psychotherapy group, it can provide an educational means for helping students integrate these negative experiences into their lives while making productive plans for the future. Process-oriented group discussion, inspired by reaction journals, is also a way for helping students empathize with those who have had very different experiences. For instructors and students who use electronic mail (E-mail), instructors may wish to make themselves available by conducting electronic office hours. Supplementing their comments to me in written reaction journals, some of my students share additional insights into the course via E-mail.

However they are designed, reaction journals have the potential of becoming transformative vehicles for creating a feminist learning community. That is, reaction journals can help make sexuality education both emotionally meaningful and intellectually stimulating. To maximize this potential, instructors should not grade or make critical intellectual comments on individual reaction journals. Instead, a small part of the student's grade in the course can be based on the number of reaction journals that were turned in on time (with gentle reminders given to those who turn in a reaction journal that neglected commentary on the daily required reading).

FEMINIST PROCESS

I strongly believe that feminist sexuality education is concerned, not just with course content, but with educational process–how students and teachers interact as human beings. If students are expected to take responsibility for their own learning and are treated as respected colleagues, the classroom becomes a more democratic place (Maher & Tetreault, 1994). At Wheaton College, for example, feminist sociologist Kersti Yllo asked her students to read Adrienne Rich's insights on "compulsory heterosexuality" (Maher & Tetrault, 1994, pp. 145-46). Yllo opened discussion with the guided image: "Imagine a system, society, or culture where we could just choose to be sexual in whatever ways we wanted, where the whole diversity of sexual choices would be celebrated. What would it be like if we didn't have that kind of compulsory aspect? . . . Yllo was pushing students to see that social norms, while comfortable for some people, are harmful to those who don't conform to them" (pp. 145-46). I have learned a great deal from Yllo's work and use a similar exercise to stimulate discussion of "heterosexual privilege" after students view a film on sexual orientation produced by gay activists.

Not all students are ready for the feminist classroom. Instead of giving up, Nancy Schniedewind (1993) describes how to teach feminist process to make feminist pedagogy work. Feminist process is based on valuing both community and equality. Emotional aspects of students' lives are valued equally with intellectual growth. For example, both the men and women I teach have written in their reaction journals or shared in class that my feminist sexuality courses "feel like group therapy or a loving family with homework." As a result of positive classroom process, my collegial relationships with some students continue into future semesters and even after they graduate.

How can feminist process be established in the classroom? First, *safety rules* are essential. In my classes, these are presented in writing and discussed with the group at the very beginning of the semester. Core to safety is the rule that students are free to talk or remain silent, that they should only share ideas they are comfortable sharing, and that all opinions and experiences are respected. Even more important, it is important for the class to discuss the importance of confidentiality. When appropriate, sexuality educators may self-disclose in the classroom, thereby equalizing power and hopefully, increasing classroom warmth. Some stories (such as the one about an unfortunate IUD that somehow "got lost" in my body) increase student comfort and add a personal dimension to our intellectual discussion. In my experience, the instructor will not be fully trusted until she or he remains accepting and open after her or his authority is first challenged by a courageous student. So, I have come to welcome that first confrontation by students. If I deal with it well, it will open up the classroom to debate and meaningful discourse like nothing else.

Schniedewind (1993) delineates the following steps to fostering feminist process in the classroom: teaching basic communication skills, providing instruction in group process skills, teaching conflict-resolution, and facilitating students' cooperation skills. I have found her ideas to have enormous practical value. After training, some of my students have handled classroom controversies and emotional outbursts better than I could on my own!

Basic communication skills. First, we need to help students learn how to identify and share feelings, own their feelings, separate thoughts from emotional reactions, and provide one another with constructive feedback. Key to this task is helping students learn how to disagree without coming across as hostile or resentful.

Group process skills. Instructors benefit from making student leadership a part of the course structure and requirements. Students may begin by brainstorming helpful roles they could take in a group (e.g., roles like the coordinator, focuser, includer, negotiator, timekeeper, and summarizer). Part of class time can be used to consider how students feel about assuming such roles as that of the process leader or constructive critic. The teacher can assign students particular roles as group discussion proceeds or simply remind them to assume leadership as needed.

Discussions of process may lead to delightful revelations. In my class recently, a student (safeguarding the true author's identity) read aloud a powerful essay on the sexual objectification of women in our culture that linked this objectification to research on sexual harassment. Students discussed this paper at length, using the word "she" to refer to the likely writer. To almost everyone's surprise, a young man declared that he had written this paper after approximately 15 minutes of class discussion. The women in class burst into spontaneous applause. "I've learned a lot about women from this class and my girlfriend," the young man reported. His disclosure was followed by that of another young man who said he was constantly correcting his fraternity brothers when they made anti-homosexual remarks or misogynistic statements about women.

Conflict resolution skills. Classes, including feminist classes, do not always go so smoothly. There are two good reasons to teach students how to resolve conflicts on their own. First, if students assist teachers in resolving conflicts, the classroom will become a safer place much sooner. Second, conflict resolution skills can generalize to students' experiences in future classes and work situations. Schniedewind (1993) rightfully points out that the teacher should not be the only one responsible for healing the group when conflict erupts. Feminist teachers can call upon the assistance of the group as a whole if disagreement takes a destructive turn. Students can be prepared for managing future conflict situations by learning the client-centered therapy technique of *reflecting feelings* (how to voice empathy for another person's disclosure or opinion), *role reversal* (purposefully voicing the other person's opinion during a conflict), and *third party mediation* (helping others resolve their disagreement satisfactorily by focusing on compromise and mutual respect). In my experience, instruction in such skills has been very helpful before students are asked to debate controversial issues such as abortion.

Increase cooperation. Feminist teachers can create structured learning activities in which small groups are responsible for a successful collective outcome and each group member is accountable for particular tasks. This is especially useful when students are expected to complete a group research project as part of the course. Two years ago, for example, some of my students increased their cooperative skills by collectively studying campus safety, including women's sexual safety. Research instruments were designed by students and each individual contributed resources for the literature review. A few students specialized in interviewing students, faculty, and public safety personnel in depth, some distributed surveys to additional students, others collected ethnographic information, and still others specialized in coding data and statistical analysis. The collaborative project, soon to be written up as a series of journal articles, gave students a valuable, "hands-on" experience with action research and group collaboration (McCormick, Nadeau, Provost, Gaeddert, & Sabo, 1996). The collective research project and collaborative experience inspired some students, who had previously thought they were best suited to "applied psychology jobs," to consider a possible future career as an active scientist or administrator of a social policy organization.

CONCLUSION

Ideally, the feminist sexuality classroom does more than provide information about sexuality; it can also inspire life goals and affirm individuals' potential for making valuable social contributions. The feminist classroom encourages students to consider the perspectives of women and other nondominant groups in their study of human sexuality. A safe environment for studying pleasure as well as coercion, the feminist classroom is also a place where instructors learn alongside their students, and everyone is invigorated by the energy of a warm and open learning community.

NOTE

1. Readers may wish to consult *Bodies besieged: The impact of chronic and serious physical illness on sexuality, passion, and desire,* a forthcoming special issue of *The Journal of Sex Research* that Naomi B. McCormick is editing for this purpose.

REFERENCES

Babb, F. E. (1994). Teaching anthropologies and sexualities. *Feminist Teacher, 8,* 119-126.

Fine, M. (1992). *Disruptive voices: The possibilities of feminist research.* Ann Arbor: University of Michigan Press.

Gussman, D., & Hesford, W. (1992). A dialogical approach to teaching introductory women's studies. *Feminist Teacher, 6,* 32-38.

Humphreys, L. (1975). *Tearoom trade: Impersonal sex in public places.* New York: Aldine De Gruyter.

Irvine, J. M. (1995). *Sexuality education across cultures: Working with differences.* San Francisco: Jossey-Bass Publishers.

Koch, P. B. (1995). *Exploring our sexuality: An interactive text.* Dubuque, IA: Kendall/Hunt Publishing Company.

Maher, F. A., & Tetreault, M. K. Thompson (1994). *The feminist classroom: An inside look at how professors and students are transforming higher education for a diverse society.* New York: Basic Books.

McCormick, N. (1992). *Students' experiences with sexual coercion and exploitation in Psychology 364A (Sex roles and sexuality): Fall 1992.* Unpublished manuscript.

McCormick, N. (1993). *Psychology 364A (Sex roles and sexuality) course outline: Spring 1993.* Unpublished manuscript.

McCormick, N. (1994a). *Sexual salvation: Affirming women's sexual rights and pleasures.* Westport, CT: Praeger.

McCormick, N. (1994b). *Psychology 364A (Sex roles and sexuality) course outline: Spring 1994.* Unpublished manuscript.

McCormick, N. (1995a). *Psychology 364A (Sex roles and sexuality) course outline: Spring 1995.* Unpublished manuscript.

McCormick, N. B. (1995b, April). Chair, Discussant, and Organizer of *Undergraduate symposium: Feminist sexuality research.* Symposium presented at the eastern region meeting of The Society for the Scientific Study of Sexuality, Atlantic City, NJ.

McCormick, N. B. (in press). Presidential Address–Our feminist future: Women affirming sexuality research in the late twentieth century. *The Journal of Sex Research.*

McCormick, N. B., & Burke, M. (1996). [Socratic pedagogy in undergraduate psychology courses. Research funded by the Outcomes Assessment Group at the State University of New York at Plattsburgh]. Unpublished raw data.

McCormick, N. B., (Chair and Discussant), Leonard, J., Santor, A., Moore, K., & Ibanez, S. (1993, November). *Images of women in computer games and the mass media.* An undergraduate research symposium presented at the meeting of The Society for the Scientific Study of Sexuality, Chicago.

McCormick, N., Nadeau, R., Provost, J., Gaeddert, W., & Sabo, A. (1996). *A multiple-method study of campus safety concerns at a four-year college.* Manuscripts for three interrelated articles in revision.

Riger, S. (1992). Epistemological debates, feminist voices: Science, social values, and the study of women. *American Psychologist, 47*, 730-740.

Samuels, H. P. (1993, June). *In the realm of the other: Sexual attitudes and behavior of black and Hispanic college students.* Plenary presented at the sixteenth annual meeting of the Eastern Region of The Society for the Scientific Study of Sexuality, Penn State University, University Park, PA.

Schniedewind, N. (1993). Teaching feminist process in the 1990s. *Women's Studies Quarterly, 21*(2 & 3), 17-30.

Shrewsbury, C. M. (1993). What is feminist pedagogy? *Women's Studies Quarterly, 21*(2 & 3), 8-16.

Stevenson, M. (1989). Creating a connected classroom: Two projects that work! *Teaching of Psychology, 16*, 212-214.

Thompson, M. E. (1993). Diversity in the classroom: Creating opportunities for learning feminist theory. *Women's Studies Quarterly, 21*(3 & 4), 113-121.

Tiefer, L. (1987). Social constructionism and the study of human sexuality. In P. Shaver and C. Hendrick (Eds.), *Sex and gender*, (pp. 70-94). Newbury Park, CA: Sage.

Tiefer, L. (1988). A feminist perspective on sexology and sexuality. In M. M. Gergen (Ed.), *Feminist thought and the structure of knowledge* (pp. 16-26). New York: New York University Press.

Tiefer, L. (1995). *Sex is not a natural act and other essays.* Boulder, CO: Westview Press.

Trudell, B. N. (1993). *Doing sex education: Gender politics and schooling.* New York: Routledge.

Wyatt, G. E. (1994). The sociocultural relevance of sex research: Challenges for the 1990s and beyond. *American Psychologist, 49*, 748-754.

Yoder, J. D., & Kahn, A. S. (1993). Working toward an inclusive psychology of women. *American Psychologist, 48*, 846-850.

APPENDIX A

Annotated Bibliography of Resources for Feminist Teachers
and Selected Biographical or Literary Materials
Useful for Feminist Sexuality Education

1. There are two journals that are of considerable interest to feminist teachers, in and outside of sexuality education, working at the elementary, secondary, and higher education level:

Feminist Teacher (published triennially by Ablex Publication Corporation. To order this journal, write: Subscription Department, Ablex Publishing Corporation, 355 Chestnut St., Norwood, NJ 07648).

Radical Teacher (published triennially by the Boston Women's Teachers Group. Write to Radical Teacher, P.O. Box 102, Kendall Square Post Office, Cambridge, MA 02142).

2. The Office of the Women's Studies Librarian, The University of Wisconsin System, publishes numerous helpful reference guides edited by Phyllis Holman Weisbard and Linda Shult. Two critical publications are: *Feminist collections: A quarterly of women's studies resources* and *Feminist Periodicals: A current listing of contents.* To order these materials, contact Phyllis Holman Weisbard, UW System Women's Studies Librarian, Room 430 Memorial Library, 728 State Street, Madison, Madison WI 53706; tel. 608 263-5754; E-mail: wiswl@macc.wis.edu

3. The most inclusive undergraduate human sexuality textbook thus far on gender, sexual orientation, and ethnicity, is a 511 page, experiential, activity-oriented book written by Patricia Barthalow Koch.

Patricia Barthalow Koch (1995). *Exploring our sexuality: An interactive text.* Dubuque, IA: Kendall/Hunt Publishing Co.

[Developed originally for the brief college course, the text could be adapted for a traditional, semester-long class if supplementary readings are assigned. Special features of this text include student activities designed to increase empathy for individuals from different sexual or ethnic groups, fact sheets, selected readings, resources, and "in their own words" narratives about a variety of sexual experiences and feelings.]

4. Three other recent sexuality books with a lot of feminist content, scientifically, theoretically, and clinically are:

Choi, L., & Nicholson, P. (Eds.). (1994). *Female sexuality: Psychology, biology, and social context.* London: Harvester Wheatsheaf.
McCormick, N. (1994). *Sexual salvation: Affirming women's sexual rights and pleasures.* Westport, CT: Praeger.
Tiefer, L. (1995). *Sex is not a natural act and other essays.* Boulder, CO: Westview Press.

5. *Nontraditional Readings: Literature, Biography, Ethnography, & History.* Students enjoy relating course content to stories of peoples' sexual lives, fictional and actual. Doing so facilitates critical thinking as well. The choice of such material is up to the teacher. *Feminist Collections,* along with book reviews in various periodicals, will keep instructors up-to-date on suitable materials. Here are a few resources I would suggest.

Delacoste, F., & Alexander, P. (Eds.). (1987). *Sex work: Writings by women in the sex industry.* Pittsburgh: Cleis Press. *[Feminist autobiographic work and essays by prostitutes and sex-club performers.]*
Donofrio, B. (1990). *Riding in cars with boys: Confessions of a bad girl who makes good.* NY: Penguin. *[This is the story of a working class, Italian-American adolescent who gets pregnant in high school; it is her story of growing up with her son. It is humorous and insightful; students love it.]*
Faderman, Lillian. (1981). *Surpassing the love of men: Romantic friendship and love between women from the Renaissance to the present.* New York: William Morrow and Company. *[Excellent historical and literary history tracing women's love letters.]*
Faderman, Lillian. (1991). *Odd girls and twilight lovers: A history of lesbian life in Twentieth-Century America.* New York: Columbia University Press. *[A classic on lesbian history although it is stronger on white, middle-class women than on women of ethnicity or working-class women.]*
Faderman, L. (Ed.) (1994). *Chloe plus Olivia: An anthology of lesbian literature from the seventeenth century to the present.* NY: Viking. *[A new book by a foremost lesbian scholar.]*
Golden, M. (Ed.) (1993). *Wild women don't wear no blues; Black women writers on love, men, and sex.* New York: Doubleday. *[These autobiographical and biographical essays and short stories by heterosexual and lesbian African-American women writers are moving and diverse in topic; students love this book and it is a good introduction to cultural diversity issues.]*

APPENDIX A (continued)

Gomez, J. (1993). *Forty-three Septembers: Essays.* Ithaca, NY: Firebrand Books. *[This is the biography of a noted, African-American lesbian writer.]*

Kennedy, E. L., & Davis, M. D. (1993). *Boots of leather, slippers of gold: The history of a lesbian community.* New York: Routledge. *[This is a powerful, historical and ethnographic study of working-class lesbians in Buffalo, NY focusing mostly on the first half of the twentieth century; the women are ethnically diverse and include Native-American and African-American lesbians.]*

Marcus, Eric. (1992). *Making history: The struggle for gay and lesbian equal rights, 1945-1990, An oral history.* New York: HarperCollins. *[Marcus interviewed pioneers of all ages in the lesbian and gay rights movement.]*

McCorvey, N. (1994). *I am Roe: My life, Roe v. Wade, and freedom of choice.* New York: HarperCollins. *[A recent recruit to the anti-choice movement, this book was written by Norma McCorvey, the anonymous Roe in the Roe v. Wade case, when she still had pro-choice sentiments. McCorvey's life story is moving. She comes from a poverty-stricken, abusive Cajun family and is now an out-lesbian, although Reproductive Rights advocates discouraged her from saying this in public initially.]*

Nestle, Joan, & Holoch, Naomi. (Eds.) (1990). *Women on women: An anthology of American lesbian short fiction.* New York: Plume. *[There are several excellent stories here. I have used many in my class but there are some which are explicitly sexual that you may want to screen before assigning. Of course, many students will read these anyway!]*

Rothblum, E. D., & Brehoney, K. A. (Eds.) (1993). *Boston marriages: Romantic but asexual relationships among contemporary lesbians.* Amherst: The University of Massachusetts Press. *[This fascinating book includes narratives by women who are passionately in love with each other but are not currently genitally active; it challenges our ideas about what sexual relationships are all about.]*

Silvera, M. (Ed.) (1992). *Piece of my heart: A lesbian of colour anthology.* Toronto: Sister Vision Press. *[This Canadian book includes many writings by lesbians from diverse ethnic backgrounds.]*

APPENDIX B

Internet Resources for Feminist Sexuality Education

1. Two articles in a recent issue of *Feminist Teacher* provide information on Internet resources for feminist instructors, including sexuality educators, that may be of interest. These articles are:

Warren-Wenk, P. (1995 Spring/Summer). Internet literacy: A guide and resources for women's studies. *Feminist Teacher, 9*(1), 6-11.

More Internet resources for feminist teachers. (1995 Spring/Summer). *Feminist Teacher, 9*(1), 12-15.

2. As clarified in Warren-Wenk's (1995) article, WMST-L, a moderated list for educators and researchers in women's studies, is one of the most valuable E-mail lists for feminist teachers, regardless of course content or academic discipline. To subscribe, send an E-mail message to: LISTSERV@UMDD.UMD.EDU

The University of Maryland maintains a gopher, InForM, which is one of the best clearinghouses for information on women and feminist teaching. This gopher includes course syllabi, conference information, bibliographies, film reviews, and general information on women. The Internet address is:

gopher://info.umd.edu:903/11/inforM/Educational_Resources/
AcademicResourcesByTopic/WomensStudies

The Women's Studies World Wide Web Site for the same information is:

http://inform.umd.edu:86/Educational_Resources/
AcademicResourcesByTopic/WomensStudies/

[This is a key web-site with many pointers to other resources.]

A User Guide to WMST-L has this URL:

http://www.unix.umbc.edu/~korenman/wmst/user-guide.html

3. A variety of additional Internet E-mail resources and lists are described below. Most of these have all been described in various issues (1993-1995) of *Feminist Collections: A Quarterly of Women's Studies Resources,* edited by Phyllis Holman Weisbard and Linda Shult. To order these materials, contact Phyllis Holman Weisbard, UW System Women's

APPENDIX B (continued)

Studies Librarian, Room 430 Memorial Library, 728 State Street, Madison, Madison WI 53706; tel. 608 263-5754; E-mail: wiswl@macc.wis.edu

Computer users can access this information via gopher or telnet to: (WiscINFO.wisc.edu). The choice, Information Databases/UW System Women's Studies Librarian's Office/Core Lists in Women's Studies will be of particular interest to readers.

Various bibliographies on a variety of topics in the field, e.g., "Lesbian Studies," are published in the series CORE LISTS IN WOMEN'S STUDIES which can be accessed via gopher or telnet to: WiscINFO.wisc.edu (and successive selections) or alternatively by opening the URL: http://www. library.wisc.edu/libraries/WomensStudies/

Please note that addresses may have changes for some of the following Internet lists since initial notices were given to the editors of *Feminist Collections: A Quarterly of Women's Studies Resources*:

CYBERSEX is a discussion list on topics such as on-line sex, erotic software, hi-tech toys, and homemade erotic videos. Subscribe by sending a message to: (LISTSERV@SOUNDPRINT.BRANDYWINE. AMERICAN.EDU). The message should ready simply *SUBSCRIBE CYBERSEX.*

FEMPED-L is a discussion list on feminist pedagogy. Send a subscribe message to: LISTSERV@UGA.CC.UGA.EDU

GLB-NEWS is a read-only, informational depository of information for gay, lesbian, bisexual, transsexual, transgender, and sympathetic persons. Subscribe to: LISTSERV@BROWNVM.BROWN.EDU

LESBIAN-STUDIES is a list for academic lesbians working in the field of lesbian studies. Membership is carefully screened. Subscribers must send a brief biographical sketch to: LESBIAN-STUDIES-APPROVAL@ NETCOM.COM

MUJER-L is an E-mail list for those interested in Chicano and/or Latina studies. Send a subscription message to: LISTPROC@LMRINET. GSE.UCSB.EDU

POWR-L is a psychology of women list for academics and researchers in the field. Send subscription requests to: POWR-L-Request@URIACC. URI.EDU

PSYCWOMEN is a list for students studying the psychology of women. Subscription messages should be sent to: PSYCWOMEN-REQUEST@ FRE.FSU.UMD.EDU

QUEER-STUDIES is a list available by sending a *subscribe* command to: QUEER-STUDIES-REQUEST@FERKEL.UCSB.EDU

SEXUAL-POLITICS carries discussions related to sexual politics. Send a *subscribe* message to: SEXUAL-POLITICS-REQUEST@REAGAN.AI. MIT.EDU

SISTAH-NET is a discussion list for African-American lesbians. Send subscription messages to: SISTAH-REQUEST@HAMP.HAMPSHIRE. EDU

STOPRAPE is a list for sexual assault activists. Subscription address is: LISTSERV@BROWNVM.BROWN.EDU

WHAM! is a women's health action and mobilization list concerned largely with reproductive rights. Subscription messages should be sent to: LISTPROC@LISTPROC.NET

Women of Color Resource Center in Berkeley, CA has this E-mail address: CHISME@IGC.APC.ORG

WMN-HLTH is a women and health list. Subscription messages should be sent to: LISTPROC@U.WASHINGTON.EDU

4. MAPSSE stands for Multidisciplinary, Academic, Professional Sexuality Students' Exploration. Housed through New York University, MAPSSE is a new, moderated, subscription only Listserv which is devoted to discussions of research, theory, and applications of information about human sexuality with a target audience of university level students. Researchers and professionals in the field are encouraged to subscribe and contribute. The goal of MAPSSE is to support student research, inquiry, program exploration, and peer evaluation.

The subscription address is: listproc@lists.nyu.edu
The message should read: subscribe mapsse Firstname Lastname
Address subsequent submissions to: mapsse@lists.nyu.edu

Controversies in Sexuality Courses at Colleges and Universities in the 1990s

Edward S. Herold, PhD

SUMMARY. Sexuality educators have always had to face issues not typically encountered by those teaching other subjects. Over the past 25 years, the general social climate at colleges and universities has been supportive of sexuality education and has had a role in shaping sexuality courses. However, contemporary higher education and the sociopolitical climate of North America now present major challenges to sexuality education, greatly complicating the role of the sexuality educator. Among the many changes in climate, the single most significant difference may be a shift away from an emphasis on providing a personally enriching experience to an emphasis on providing a personally safe environment for all students. The implications of this are briefly discussed and illustrated. *[Article copies available for a fee from The Haworth Document Delivery Service: 1-800-342-9678. E-mail address: getinfo@haworth.com]*

Is sexuality education at the college or university level more difficult these days? Have the controversies associated with such teaching changed over the past several decades? To what extent are

---

Edward S. Herold is affiliated with the Department of Family Studies, University of Guelph.

Address correspondence to Edward S. Herold, Department of Family Studies, University of Guelph, Guelph, Ontario, Canada, N1G 2W1.

[Haworth co-indexing entry note]: "Controversies in Sexuality Courses at Colleges and Universities in the 1990s." Herold, Edward S. Co-published simultaneously in *Journal of Psychology & Human Sexuality* (The Haworth Press, Inc.) Vol. 9, No. 3/4, 1997, pp. 71-86; and: *Sexuality Education in Postsecondary and Professional Training Settings* (ed: James W. Maddock) The Haworth Press, Inc., 1997, pp. 71-86. Single or multiple copies of this article are available for a fee from The Haworth Document Delivery Service [1-800-342-9678, 9:00 a.m. - 5:00 p.m. (EST). E-mail address: getinfo@haworth.com].

71

sexuality educators aware of the potential trouble spots in their courses? In exploring these issues, I will use my 25 years of experience teaching sexuality courses, as well as 16 years chairing one of the major North American sexuality conferences. In addition, I have had the opportunity for numerous discussions with colleagues about teaching sexuality courses in a wide variety of higher education settings.

One thing is clear: Sexuality continues to be a controversial subject; therefore, it presents a unique educational challenge. Being well-prepared as a teacher is important, but it is not enough. Because the controversies surrounding sexuality courses are greater than for most other curriculum areas, having a supportive administration makes teaching this subject much easier–and allows the instructor freedom to be more innovative and effective.

When I first began teaching a human sexuality course in 1971, the major concern was whether the subject of sex was sufficiently "academic" to be offered as a credit course. At that time, there were only a couple of textbooks from which to choose and only one research journal specializing in sexuality. In the years since, the amount of sex-related research has exploded, as have the number of sexuality textbooks and journals. Today, even the most exceptional sexuality educator will find it challenging to keep up with the relevant research and other materials.

SEXUALITY EDUCATION AS PERSONAL ENRICHMENT

Depending upon the academic background of the instructor as well as the department or curriculum area in which a sexuality course is located, sexuality education can be approached in a variety of ways. However, the relevance of sexuality to personal life leads most educators and textbook writers to include objectives, teaching materials, and learning experiences aimed at student *self-awareness and personal development*. In the early 1970s, an emphasis on "personal growth" was especially strong, perhaps as a result of the significance of "self-actualization" and "interpersonal encounter" in the cultural climate of that time, particularly in North America's colleges and universities.

Advocates of this approach encouraged sexuality educators to be role models for openness and comfort by, among other things, giving personal examples from their own sexual development and experience. Class assignments also were designed to encourage self-assessment. Self-analysis papers, in which students examined their own sexual backgrounds and personal development, were often used either as required or optional assignments. Sexuality professionals (as well as other educators and clinicians) were encouraged, even mandated, to participate in "sexual attitude reassessment" (SAR) workshops that included sexually explicit films, small group sharing sessions, and presentations by individuals representing a variety of atypical sexual lifestyles. Annual meetings of the major sexuality organizations frequently included SARs and other workshops dealing with participants' personal attitudes, feelings, and values about various aspects of sexuality. The underlying assumption of these experiences and of a variety of educational activities was that sexuality educators, as well as other health and helping professionals, need to be conscious of how their own sexual attitudes and beliefs influence their teaching and counselling.

Over the years, one of the most popular activities in college sexuality courses has focused on awareness and comfort with sexual terminology. In class, students might be asked to shout out synonyms and slang terms for genitals and for various sexual activities. Alternately, students might be divided into small groups that compete at drawing up lists of such terms. These exercises highlight some of the difficulties of communicating about sexuality, and they also act as social icebreakers among students.

In the 1970s, the use of sexually explicit films in college classrooms was controversial, though gaining acceptance. A number of sexuality educators argued that realistic portrayals of sexual anatomy and physiology, as well as depictions of erotic activities, added an important dimension to their educational efforts. If factual films about a variety of subjects could be shown in other courses, why not take advantage of high quality instructional materials in sexuality courses as well? Generally, college and university students accepted and appreciated these explicit media in their courses. Nevertheless, a common concern among sexuality educators was the risk of losing the support of their administrators if controversy about these films arose from *outside* of the classroom. Indeed, occasional controversies did arise, and some administrators expressed concern, although most backed their faculty on the basis of academic freedom and educational legitimacy.

Accompanying the emphasis on personal growth in sexuality education (at all levels) was the expanded role of the classroom educator. Because sexuality educators were perceived to be open and nonjudgmental, students in sexuality courses often felt more comfortable talking with their course instructors about a sexual concern rather than going to see school counsellors or other helping professionals. In their text on sexuality education, for example, Bruess and Greenberg (1988) argued for the legitimacy of sexuality educators (with appropriate personal characteristics) serving as counsellors to students in their courses–although they recognized that some sex-related personal problems are clearly outside the domain of the educator.

In summary, the personal growth orientation of the social and behavioral sciences clearly has had a major influence on the teaching of human sexuality in college and university classrooms. An excellent review of the rationale for this orientation, as well as a discussion of relevant teaching strategies, is presented by Delamater, Hyde, and Allgeier (1994). Except for periodic complaints from religiously conservative students or others who disapprove of certain educational techniques (such as the use of explicit films) or an occasional assertion by some academicians that sexuality education courses lack intellectual rigor, the general consensus among sexuality educators has been that personal enrichment objectives and experiences are a valuable part of the sexuality curriculum.

THE CURRENT CLIMATE

Beginning in the 1980s and increasing in the 1990s, new questions have been raised concerning the teaching approaches and techniques used in university sexuality courses. While these questions have come from various sources, feminist groups have played a major role. Naomi McCormick (1997) does an excellent job of summarizing feminist principles and outlining how they can modify the teaching of human sexuality. However, there are some problems that can arise as a result of adopting the approach she advocates, as well as some issues that her analysis leaves unresolved.

Most significant, in my view, is a subtle but significant shift in focus from an emphasis on personal development and empowerment to an emphasis on protecting students from the possibilities of various forms of sexual victimization. As a result, educators are required to adopt a more cautious approach to dealing with the inherently personal ramifications of sexuality. The implication is that instructors must carefully search all of their materials to insure against the possibility of offending any students. The risk is that a negative aura is once again created around the subject of sexuality—either eliminate potentially offensive materials or "warn" students ahead of time that such offenses may occur.

In the immediate context of a given class session in a given course, such precautions may be appropriate. However, in the current climate of higher education, such a stance has more far-reaching implications. In recent discussions with colleagues in other academic fields, I have learned that many are avoiding issues related to sexuality in their courses. Repeatedly, I have heard male faculty members state that they now avoid references to the topic of sexuality in their courses in order to reduce the possibility of being accused of sexual harassment. Similarly, discussions of sexuality in mixed company outside the classroom are also evaded for the same reason. Certainly, nothing that I am saying should be construed as supporting sexual harassment in any form. However, I am concerned that the implications of some aspects of "political correctness" in relation to gender can contribute to returning communication about sexuality to tabooed status in North America. What are the implications of this for sexuality educators? One danger is that interests in sexual topics, including enrolling in academic sexuality courses, could again be seen as "deviant," a stereotype that sexuality educators have struggled long and hard to overcome (Maddock, 1997).

Over the years, I have asked students about the reactions of their friends and families when they announce their enrollment in a sexuality course. Predictably, the question elicits a variety of responses. I continue to be unpleasantly surprised at how many students report that others are interested, but also shocked, to hear about the topics dealt with in a sexuality course. I believe that students should not have to defend their decision to take a sexuality course at the college level, nor should they have to undergo intense scrutiny if they wish to pursue study in the field beyond an introductory course. A student seriously considering graduate study in human sexuality recently told me that she found virtually no support in her community for her interest. The student revealed that the negative reaction of others led her to wait two years before she could muster enough courage to apply to several university graduate programs that focused on human sexuality.

CLASSROOM MATERIALS

In addition to the more general context of higher education, there have been significant changes in classroom climate within sexuality courses themselves. Some of these are for the better. For example, diversity in sexual behavior is receiving more attention than ever before. Further, recognition is being given to how certain sexual issues, such as sexual harassment and date rape, affect everyday life rather than framing these as sexual problems involving "perverted" individuals in isolated or bizarre circumstances. But problems have also accompanied the emergence of the new pedagogy in sexuality education.

First is the matter of using sexually explicit films–or almost any form of audiovisual material–as teaching aids. No longer does the course content automatically justify the appropriateness of certain materials. Rather, the value of each piece of media must be weighed against the possibility that one or more students might be offended by it. A number of faculty, including widely recognized, highly respected instructors in popular courses, have decided that the political risks of using certain materials is simply too great.

Related to this is the matter of prior warning to students about explicit or potentially offensive or emotional material or discussions in the classroom, once again raising the *in loco parentis* issue so long debated on college campuses and familiar to sexuality educators at all educational levels. What should be required and what should be optional? How can appropriate cautions be given without setting a negative tone? When and how should students be given an opportunity to "opt out" of certain parts of a course or particular classroom experiences–or even to waive an entire course requirement?

Over the past decade, it has become accepted convention in most college and university classrooms to inform students in writing at the beginning of the course that sexually explicit depictions are to be used. Additional warnings are then issued at the time a particular film or video is to be shown. Often, students are informed that they may leave the class when these films are shown; sometimes, they are assured that the potentially controversial material will not be used in any way for exams or other forms of student evaluation. The objective seems clear: Instructors want to protect students from possible discomfort, or even harm, that such exposure might produce–or do they simply want to avoid complaints and legal challenges? What message is being sent, and what values are reflected? This procedure singles out sexual portrayals as most likely to cause offense, reflecting society's ongoing ambivalence about sexuality and a continuing emphasis on sexual hazard over sexual health (Maddock, 1997).

A few years ago, in response to student complaints that erotic films had been shown in several classes (though not a sexuality course), the Iowa Board of Regents imposed a disclaimer policy on all course content, requiring all faculty to warn students before using any kind of sexually explicit materials which could be considered offensive (Leatherman, 1993). Thus, Iowa students have the option of either not attending classes when explicit images are shown or of not taking a particular course due to its sexual content.

At a university in New Mexico, however, such prior warnings were insufficient to protect the instructor of a sexuality course from administrative censure. At the beginning of the term, the faculty member informed students that sexually explicit materials would be used; students were alerted again at the beginning of each class period in which films were shown. Nevertheless, a student complained to the administration that he had not been warned in an appropriate way–that is, at the *prior* class period–and found it too embarrassing to leave the classroom before the materials were used. The administration sided with the student, and the instructor was reprimanded.

INSTRUCTIONAL METHODS

Like explicit films, certain teaching methods also may now be considered offensive. For example, a new faculty member at a university in the southern U.S. recently used the class exercise on generating synonyms for genitals and sexual activities. While most students clearly appreciated the exercise, one student was offended by the use of such "crude" language and complained to the college dean. The dean admonished the professor and warned him that this exercise must never again be used in the course.

Even having students engage in activities designed to examine controversial sexual issues can create problems. For example, a Professor of Law at a Canadian university instructed his students to prepare legal arguments for and against a hypothetical antipornography law, asking them to adopt a point of view other than their own. Some of the students were upset about having to argue against their own beliefs, and they complained to the university's sexual harassment officer. The harassment officer subsequently warned the instructor that a repeat of the exercise could lead to a sexual harassment investigation (Fekete, 1994).

Conducting class surveys on attitudes, beliefs, and behaviors of students, and comparing these with large scale research studies, has long been standard operating procedure in college sexuality courses. However, some institutional research ethics committees have raised questions about whether it is appropriate for an instructor to survey the sexual attitudes and behaviors of students in one's own course, even though this is typically done with complete anonymity. In the name of "protecting" students, an opportunity for increased self-awareness and insight may be lost. Overly restrictive ethics committees may also discourage student projects that involve field research of any kind. In my courses, students interested in conducting a survey or some interviews to fulfill a term assignment often change their minds when told that they must submit approval forms to the Ethics Review Committee. Clearly, there are benefits to such requirements. Among other things, students learn about the general guidelines and technical procedures for ethical research. Likewise, faculty doing sexuality education are reminded of the importance of following institutional procedures–and of the continuing controversial nature of sex research. At the same time, it is important to recognize that some members of ethics committees may have a particular bias against sexuality research. Given the current political climate of universities, they may now have an easier time in blocking this research.

Such restrictions and cautions can also affect the basic direction of sexuality education at the college level. Should courses encourage exploration and discussion of personal sexual issues? James Barbour (1989) has described an assignment used in an introductory sexuality course. Students are asked to write a "sexual development paper," which is reviewed and graded by student assistants (senior undergraduates enrolled in an advanced sexuality course). The paper is to cover the following topics: the self as female/male, the self as sexual, body image, sexual experience, and sexual orientation. Barbour believes that the various safeguards he has put into place nullify any significant risks to students related to this assignment. On the other hand, assigning such personal papers has been criticized, even when the assignments are voluntary (e.g., Swartzlander, Pace & Stamier, 1993). One question raised is whether it is appropriate at all for instructors–not to mention other students–to grade papers dealing with personal subjects that may be emotionally charged for some of those who write them. Another concern is that students who feel shameful about some of their past experiences might be further traumatized by writing about them (even though they have not been specifically requested to do so).

McCormick (1997) correctly observes that appropriate self-disclosure by a course instructor can increase the comfort level of students through positive modelling. Certainly, this has been the prevailing belief among sexuality educators–at least until recently. Increasingly, however, the opposite point of view is being voiced; namely, that stories of personal life experiences revealed by sexuality educators may threaten students or make them uncomfortable. For example, Swartzlander et al. (1993) cite as "inappropriate" the revelation by an instructor of the incestuous abuse in her own childhood.

In today's climate of increased awareness of sexual harassment, having personal discussions of any kind in the context of college courses can be risky, even when there is no suggestion of anything as inappropriate as sexual advances or physical contact. For example, Jane Gallop (1994), who teaches courses on feminism, has described her experience of being charged with sexual harassment by two female graduate students. After investigating the complaints, the affirmative action office at her university chastised her for conducting discussions that were "too personal." Gallop criticizes such a stance, in part because it runs counter to some of the very tenets of feminist scholarship, such as affirming subjective experience and making explicit one's personal frame of reference for understanding social phenomena.

Recently, I have noticed that this concern about focusing on personal experience in the context of sexuality education is not limited to the higher education context. Even meetings of sexuality professionals–at which there is a long tradition of recognizing the interplay between the personal and professional–have begun to reflect a more negative form of protectionism. Not long ago, I attended a personal development workshop at a national conference, during which several participants objected to the use of a dyadic exercise in which they were asked to share in private discussion with one other participant any childhood or adolescent event that had a significant impact on their subsequent sexual development. The objectors expressed their discomfort with being asked to share any personal experiences in a workshop context. What interested me was the fact that these individuals had voluntarily enrolled in a workshop whose focus on personal development was clearly stated. The two workshop leaders appeared to be puzzled by the challenge and reiterated the voluntary nature of the experience, after which the workshop proceeded–and most participants completed the exercise. More than anything, this reinforced for me the changing atmosphere of sexuality education: Protection against potential harm apparently has replaced motivation for personal insight and growth as the top priority of educators.

TENSIONS SURROUNDING DIVERSITY AND INCLUSIVENESS

Another issue widely discussed within the academic community in the past two decades has been the dominance of white males and the distinct minority status of women and persons of color, as well as of gay males and lesbians. Several other authors in this volume describe why special efforts need to be made in sexuality courses to

ensure that the voices of diversity and the concerns of disadvantaged groups are recognized and addressed. Such issues have become increasingly visible in sexuality courses over the past few
years, and there can be no argument about the importance of dealing
with diversity in the field of sexuality. However, just how to do this
in both equitable and effective ways is more troublesome. Precisely
what balance should be struck between a focus on issues that may
be important to one group, but not to another? How much time and
energy should be devoted to subjects that may be rather unique to a
small number of individuals versus those of more general concern?
For example, if 90% of the students in a course identify themselves
as heterosexual, should instructors plan to use heterosexual examples 90% of the time, or should they strive for an equal balance
between heterosexual and homosexual illustrations? Increasingly,
gay male and lesbian students are requesting or demanding "equal
representation" in sexuality courses. Particularly since 1990, I have
noticed a dramatic increase in the number of comments by participants at the annual Guelph Conference on Sexuality complaining
that conference speakers were "heterosexist," "noninclusive," "too
marriage-focused," or "used tokenist language in referring to same
sex relationships." Many of the speakers at this conference have
been well-known, highly experienced, interpersonally skilled sexuality educators. Whatever may be the particulars of a given presentation, the solution to speaking inclusively to the concerns of a
diverse audience is certainly a major challenge today. Clearly, sexuality educators face enormous difficulties in their attempts to be
inclusive in the classroom.

   McCormick (1997) also notes the shortcomings likely to exist in
sexuality courses with regard to issues of racial and ethnic diversity.
In recent years, an increasing number of students (and academic
scholars) have claimed that comparisons among various groups are
inherently racist and should never be made, especially when such
comparisons appear to disadvantage a particular group. They argue
that certain statistical comparisons are inherently biased against
minorities, for example, the data indicating that more African-
American teenagers have unplanned births than do those in other
ethnic groups. Some students even contend that the presentation of

such findings in a classroom or a textbook reflects the "systemic racism" to be found in all of higher education.

In her article, McCormick (1997) summarizes steps that can be taken to acknowledge and address the dignity of all groups in the context of recognizing diversity. However, it appears that many faculty, including sexuality educators, are most likely to yield to the temptation to "play it safe" by avoiding any references to minority groups or omitting research findings that might be politically contro- versial, except for those which are critical of mainstream North American culture. One instructor with whom I spoke admitted go- ing out of his way in a discussion of cultural differences to empha- size that sex education in the United States and Canada is clearly inferior to that in the Scandinavian countries–the only intergroup comparison he felt it safe to make.

To take the dilemma a step further, we might ask whether hetero- sexual males as a group are currently welcome in human sexuality courses on college campuses? How can their concerns be appropri- ately represented in such courses? How should stereotypes about male sexuality be dealt with? Because most of the students in cam- pus sexuality courses are women, male students often report feeling distinctly like a disadvantaged minority, fearful of revealing them- selves or of saying the "wrong thing." The number of males in my sexuality course has decreased over the years, as has the level of contributions made by those men who do enroll.

Should this be a cause for concern? Are we in danger of returning to the days of de facto segregation in the classroom, when certain courses in areas such as home economics or family life were viewed as "women's courses" and, therefore, irrelevant–perhaps even an- tagonistic–to men? A self-described feminist writer, journalist Wendy Dennis (1992) conducted a survey of men's and women's concerns regarding dating and sexual relationships. Dennis reported that, as a result of interviewing the men for her survey, she developed greater sympathy for the problems of males. She concluded that many contemporary men may be suffering emotionally as much as women have, and men are as confused as women about how to relate effectively to the other sex. Unfortunately, Dennis also noted that she was bitterly attacked by some radical feminists for showing too much sympathy toward men. Yet, unfair stereotypes of men abound, and they are reflected in today's popular culture to the same degree and with the same negativity that once characterized the stereotypes of women that we now claim to abhor. And most men do not fit the stereotypes–particularly the males who voluntarily enroll in college sexuality courses.

Like McCormick and most other faculty who teach sexuality courses, I believe that such courses should be concerned with respecting all groups and addressing the needs of all individuals. But the question remains: How can it be done equitably? Women in sexuality courses typically want equal attention given to both genders (as do males). Indeed, women at my university have consistently indicated that they wish more men would enroll in sexuality courses and would participate more actively when they attend classes. Similarly, students tend to desire more exposure to cultural and ethnic diversity on sex-related topics; naturally, however, no one wants to have his/her own identity or experience unrecognized or belittled. That is human nature, but the inevitable biases and fears that are also part of human nature make the challenge of inclusive and respectful sexuality education a formidable one.

Finally, there is the matter of gender and "political correctness," even among sexuality educators. In today's climate, male instructors appear to be under great scrutiny regarding potentially inappropriate comments or actions in the context of sexuality courses. Some female students (and faculty) seem to consider offensive behavior by males inevitable, and they stand ever ready to challenge and "correct" the errant individual. One faculty member at a university in the U.S. related an incident involving a female colleague (with whom he sometimes teaches family and sexuality courses): When he challenged her public labelling of all males in the family field as "sexist, inconsiderate, and insensitive," she rebuked him with the comment that perhaps the men in her own department might be at least "one step above the men [she] would meet at a truck stop." Are such pejorative characterizations any more acceptable when they come from a member of a sometimes disadvantaged group? Or have we reached a point in time where it has become acceptable to label all men as the "inferior sex"? Sexuality educators are challenged to help students of both sexes prepare for their future lives as adults, partners, parents, and citizens in a society that sometimes seems like a gender war zone.

In recent years I have had many informal discussions with a variety of faculty from universities throughout North America regarding how the issue of gender might affect instructors in sexuality courses. Many are convinced that male sexuality educators are currently given much less latitude than females for conducting wide ranging discussions, airing their views on issues, and using creative teaching techniques. Delamater, Hyde, and Allgeier (1994) argue that male sexuality instructors are at a disadvantage in that some of classroom exercises "may be carried out more safely (in regard to possible charges of impropriety or harassment) by a woman than by a man" (p. 310). In fact, one of the authors (Elizabeth Rice Allgeier), a well-known and highly regarded sexuality educator and researcher, has publicly stated her belief that she has considerably more freedom to be open in her personal comments than does her husband, also a recognized sexuality educator.

At the same time, the current climate of higher education surely places restrictions on faculty of *both* genders. In California, a male student threatened to file a $2.5 million lawsuit in connection with a sexual harassment charge against a female faculty member who gave a guest lecture on sexuality in an introductory psychology course. The student complained that the instructor had engaged in "crude, unadulterated male-bashing" (*Wall Street Journal*, 1995). The student complainant in this case identified himself as "a Christian." While this may have been germane to the particulars of that situation, it may also signal the beginning of a trend in which political conservatives will use established human rights policies to charge those whose views differ from their own.

CONCLUSION

Because sexuality is such an emotionally-laden and controversial subject, strong differences of opinion about appropriate teaching methods and materials will no doubt continue to exist. Some instructors believe that they may reduce their chances of being criticized by focusing a course exclusively on research findings and not dealing at all with personal issues. However, even this strategy still leaves the instructor open to accusations. At a university in Chicago, an instructor was accused of sexual harassment because of his comparison of gender differences in a sexuality course. Although the charges were dropped, the instructor was so traumatized by the experience that he now refuses to teach a sexuality course and will not discuss research on gender differences in any of his other courses.

To provide sexuality education without offending someone at sometime is probably impossible. However, this problem must be kept in perspective, because the overwhelming majority of college students are *not* upset at what and how they are taught in sexuality courses. For the most part, they appreciate the challenge of learning more about themselves and about the subject matter.

Developing clear educational policies and course conduct guidelines can be an effective means of dealing with heightened concerns over issues of personal privacy and emotional safety. Students should be reminded about the human rights policies of their institution. Further, the goals of recognition and respect for diversity, and even disagreement, should be made clear at the beginning of the course. Students should be specifically informed of their privacy rights, and these should be related clearly to course procedures such as the writing of diaries or personal papers, small group discussion, and viewing of explicit media. Making comprehensive and detailed information available is both a legal safeguard and a sign of respect for the students as individuals. Within the limits of broader academic policies, students may decide if they wish to enroll in a sexuality course and how they wish to participate in the course to meet its requirements. In addition, students should always be provided with information about resources for personal problem solving if the need should arise. But, they should also be informed that they cannot be artificially protected from all forms of emotional stress or personal offense when they choose to take a sexuality course.

My major objective in this article has been to make explicit some of the new challenges and dilemmas facing those teaching sexuality courses in colleges and universities. The examples I have given indicate that, in some respects, sexuality courses have become more difficult to teach. By giving voice to these challenges, I hope to encourage others to speak out, to discuss and debate, and to work together on finding solutions. Often, faculty teaching sexuality courses have no one among their everyday colleagues with whom to share these concerns. This makes it all the more necessary for academic and professional sexuality organizations and publications to provide opportunities for discussing these issues. After all, isn't communicating meaningfully one of the most important goals of effective sexuality education?

REFERENCES

Barbour, J. R. (1989). Teaching a course in human relationships and sexuality: A model for personalizing large groups instruction. *Family Relations, 38,* 142-148.

Bruess, C. E., and Greenberg, J. S. (1988). *Sexuality education.* New York: Macmillan.

Delamater, J., Hyde, J., and Allgeier, E. (1994). Teaching human sexuality: Personalizing the impersonal lecture. *Teaching Sociology, 22,* 309-318.

Dennis, W. (1992). *Hot and bothered: Love and sex in the 90's.* Toronto: Seal.

Fekete, J. (1994). *Moral panic: Biopolitics rising.* Toronto: Robert Davies.

Gallop, J. (1994). Feminism and harassment policy. *Academe, 80,* 16-23.

Leatherman, C. (December 8, 1993). Dealing with sexual images in Iowa classrooms. *The Chronicle of Higher Education, 39,* A22, 24.

Maddock, J. W. (1997). Sexuality education: A history lesson. *Journal of Psychology & Human Sexuality, 9* (3/4), 1-22.

McCormick, N. B. (1997). Celebrating diversity: Feminist sexuality education in the undergraduate classroom. *Journal of Psychology & Human Sexuality, 9* (3/4), 37-69.

Swartzlander, S., Pace, D., and Stamier, V. (February 17, 1993). The ethics of requiring students to write about their personal lives. *The Chronicle of Higher Education, 39,* B1-2.

Wall Street Journal (1995). Was prof's lecture academic freedom or sex harassment? March 7; 1.

The Failure of Sexuality Education: Meeting the Challenge of Behavioral Change in a Sex-Positive Context

Dennis M. Dailey, DSW

SUMMARY. Even "comprehensive" sexuality education has failed to reach its potential in that it cannot convincingly demonstrate its effectiveness in facilitating behavioral change. Commitment to a comprehensive, sex-positive perspective is proposed as one important component in creating behavioral outcomes that balance the reduction of hurt with the enhancement of pleasure. Until sexuality educators become comfortable and committed to emphasizing the pleasure dimension of sexual experience, the legitimate impact of sexuality education may be compromised in the eyes of students. *[Article copies available for a fee from The Haworth Document Delivery Service: 1-800-342-9678. E-mail address: getinfo@haworth.com]*

In many ways, sexuality education has not lived up to its potential for reducing human hurt and enhancing human pleasure. As generally conceived and delivered in the United States, it has large-

---

Dennis M. Dailey is affiliated with the School of Social Welfare at the University of Kansas.

Address correspondence to Dennis M. Dailey, School of Social Welfare, University of Kansas, Twente Hall, Lawrence, KS 66045-2510.

[Haworth co-indexing entry note]: "The Failure of Sexuality Education: Meeting the Challenge of Behavioral Change in a Sex-Positive Context." Dailey, Dennis M. Co-published simultaneously in *Journal of Psychology & Human Sexuality* (The Haworth Press, Inc.) Vol. 9, No. 3/4, 1997, pp. 87-97; and: *Sexuality Education in Postsecondary and Professional Training Settings* (ed: James W. Maddock) The Haworth Press, Inc., 1997, pp. 87-97. Single or multiple copies of this article are available for a fee from The Haworth Document Delivery Service [1-800-342-9678, 9:00 a.m. - 5:00 p.m. (EST). E-mail address: getinfo@haworth.com].

87

ly failed to meet its own (admittedly ambitious) goals. Specifically, sexuality education has not had demonstrable success at affecting the *behavior* of recipients. In a time when sexual dysfunction and dissatisfaction in primary relationships still occur with much frequency, focusing on behavioral change to enhance pleasure continues to be important. In an age of HIV/AIDS and other health-endangering and life-risking consequences, focusing on behavioral change to reduce hurt is particularly crucial.

Most educators claim to possess some form of theory about learning that guides their teaching efforts. There is widespread agreement that the education/learning process has at least three essential components, none of which is inherently more important than another. Most simply stated, these components are: *knowledge* (cognitive mastery of factual materials); *attitudes/values* (preferences or beliefs about what ought to be); and *skills* (behaviors resulting from, and connected to, knowledge and values) (Dailey, 1975b). Sexuality educators tend to agree that the most effective education/ learning process is not complete without addressing each of these components. The concept of comprehensive sexuality education reflects this emphasis.

Each of the three components is important, and balance between them needs to be achieved; however, there may be some logical progression that applies in the education/learning process. Classroom observation makes it clear that the priority given these components significantly affects the teaching strategies of sexuality educators (among others). For example, many of the curricula developed by ideological conservatives place a strong emphasis on attitudes and values, with lesser emphasis on knowledge, and almost complete lack of attention to behavioral expressions other than abstinence. By contrast, much sexuality education in public school settings gives uneven attention to knowledge acquisition, with little or no emphasis on attitudes and values, and is reluctant to deal at all with behavioral expression.

MODELS OF EDUCATION/LEARNING

Some educators emphasize what might be called a *learning by doing* model. For example, clinical trainers often assert that one cannot learn how to do therapy from a book, but only from actual experience. Such thinking is the rationale behind practicum and internship experiences that are part of the training of learners in professional programs, both clinical and educational. Crucial to this model is the notion of "hands-on learning." Experience is the teacher, and the student is challenged to infer what is to be learned from the experience itself. Educators will recognize this as an inductive model of learning; that is, inferring from specific experiences to a variety of more general concepts and principles.

A second model might be termed *learning for doing*. In this approach, cognitive mastery precedes action; that is, knowing comes before doing. Advocates of this approach argue that classroom learning and assessment of cognitive mastery must occur before meaningful change in real life behaviors can take place. Of course, this is the deductive approach to education/learning, in which a given behavior is understood as a singular exemplar of a larger theoretical schema.

A third model, *learning by/for doing*, reflects a dialectical synthesis of the other two. In this educational approach, knowledge acquisition and cognitive mastery may occur prior to action or application. However, application is valued as an equally important part of the learning process in that it validates both knowledge and values by directly demonstrating their relevance to behavior. In the dialectical approach, there is continuous feedback between knowledge, values, and behaviors–each influencing and being influenced by the other (Gordon and Schutz, 1969).

The first two models summarized above tend to be linear in nature, whereas the third is more systemic and better captures the complex dynamics of human experience. For that very reason, however, the third model is more challenging to manage in the education/learning context, which may account for its being less often used by educators as a guide to classroom activities. To date, sexuality education reflects primarily a *learning for doing* approach, even though educators recognize that children and adolescents tend to learn most about sexuality from their own direct experiences.

In the many studies that have examined the acquisition of knowledge about sexuality, parents and schools are seldom reported to be the primary sources of information. Rather, friends (who themselves are poorly informed) or interpersonal experiences serve as the primary sources of information. As a result, young people are often forced into blind experimentation because there are few options available to them that will respectfully nurture healthy sexual development.

Some educators utilize a limited version of a *learning by/for doing* approach by providing students with information about the behavioral implications of their knowledge and values. Unfortunately, this reflects the realm of "knowledge about" rather than the internalized reality of learned experience. Knowledge for its own sake is not without value; however, the powerful reality of human sexuality demands attention to its concrete implications for life. The linear expectation that knowledge will lead automatically to behavioral change is seldom demonstrated.

The *learning by/for doing* model supports a balanced relationship between knowledge, attitudes and values, and behavior, as well as reflecting a logical progression in the education/learning process. For example, many sexuality educators would prefer that some knowledge be acquired early in the learning process. It is not anticipated that one should "know everything" prior to any sort of sexual experience; rather, knowledge should be sufficient to minimize negative outcomes and enhance positive ones. One may eventually choose to accept or reject what is known, but *finding out* what is known should be considered important. Likewise, it is important for students to learn to use their experiences as feedback that can confirm or disconfirm their baseline knowledge, as well as to motivate the quest for enriching that knowledge, and to further challenge attitudes and/or values so that these may be altered or held with greater conviction.

In the process of education/learning, attitude and value stances may derive from knowledge, or they may evolve independent of verified facts (as in the case of ethical dictates from any one of many chosen belief systems). One may know all that is to be known about HIV/AIDS, premarital sexual intercourse, masturbation, oral sex, or homosexuality; yet, on the basis of personal beliefs, attitudes, or values, one may reject what is known in favor of his/her preference for how things *ought* to be. For example, considerable data indicate no appreciable difference in the psychological health of heteroerotic and homoerotic individuals; however, this information is rejected by those who believe that homosexuality is *prima facie* an illness (Dailey, 1975a; Bell and Weinberg, 1978; Sagier and Robins, 1973). Similarly, one's belief that masturbation is a sin may lead one to reject the statistics on its incidence throughout the life cycle. Or one's belief that HIV/AIDS is God's retribution for homosexuality may create a false sense of security in a heterosexual individual (Greenspan and Castro, 1990).

There is little question that the attitudes/values issue is a delicate one, almost as threatening to some as the issue of behavioral expression. Attitude/value clarification can be a part of the educational process, but it is often neglected by educators out of fear of what parents or others outside the educational context may think about the effort. Challenges such as "Are they teaching the *right* things?" or "I don't want my kids learning some values that I don't agree with!" understandably threaten sexuality educators and may result in watered-down teaching efforts. For example, the thrust of mandated sex and HIV/AIDS education over the past decade may actually have increased the number of teachers who are not well-trained and/or do not really want to be teaching this subject matter (Krueger, 1991; Reed and Munson, 1976). This problem becomes even more acute as state mandated sexuality education is being challenged, severely altered, or withdrawn entirely (Ross and Kantor, 1995).

What continues to be most difficult to make clear and convincing is that teaching a particular value system and creating a context in which students can search and find their own values are two very *different* processes. For example, students in my university sexuality classes typically have few serious disagreements related to sexual information, but they frequently argue about ideas and attitudes, reflecting a desire to discover and solidify their own values. As long as there is a fundamental commitment to respect diversity of opinion, each individual's search can be successful.

Clearly, knowledge and values are intertwined in the education/ learning process. Attitudes and values not only dictate whether knowledge is accepted or rejected; they influence how information itself is understood, i.e., the process of knowing. Of course, knowledge also influences attitudes and values. Attitudes may change or be reinforced by what comes to be known. For example, some parents alter their negative attitudes towards sex education when they learn that comprehensive, positive sexuality education can result in such things as delayed experience with sexual intercourse or reduced pregnancy rates.

TRANSLATIONS INTO BEHAVIOR

The third component of education/learning is the actual behavior (i.e., skills) that reflects what is known and what is valued by the educator and/or student. The correct use of a condom during sexual intercourse is an example of a "sexual skill." Obviously, knowing nothing at all about condoms will result in their not being used. However, having knowledge of condoms but believing their use to be sinful or thinking that they interfere with sexual pleasure may also result in nonuse. Further, it is possible to know all about condoms, have no attitude or value conflicts regarding their use, but still not use them (or misuse them), based upon behavioral deficits resulting from experiential unfamiliarity. This is vividly illustrated by the current paradox of sexuality education programs that mandate knowledge of sexually transmitted diseases such as AIDS, but forbid discussion of sexual behaviors that place individuals at risk for HIV transmission or of preventive techniques (Kantor, 1992). The classic "catch-22" for today's young people is knowledge of danger with no behavioral translations or options. Perhaps this helps account for the lack of behavioral outcome evaluation in most sexuality education programs (Kirby, 1984, 1985). Examining such outcomes presupposes that a significant number of students will demonstrate the behavior that is being evaluated. And some sexuality educators are uncomfortable acknowledging and discussing the behavioral implications of their work precisely *because* they fear a negative response by parents, administrators, or others.

A variety of classroom activities can be used to link knowledge to behavior. For example, students in my courses may be asked to purchase condoms and bring them to class along with a banana or other penis substitute. The presence of large zucchinis, baseball bats, flash lights, and the like not only lend some humor to the experience, but may lead to useful discussion of male concern about penis size. I have sometimes had students practice putting a condom both on their own bananas and on bananas held by classmates. These two experiences often produce very different reactions in students and subtly different behavioral experiences.

Sometimes, I ask student volunteers to role play various scenarios regarding condom use in typical social situations. For example, a man and woman from the class might be instructed to role play two sexually experienced individuals who have been dating a short time and decide to have intercourse, but must first discuss protective measures. Or two males may be asked to be a gay couple ready to become more genitally active with each other. Or two women may be asked to play a lesbian couple at the time one first reveals to the other that she has active herpes and needs to consider protection for her partner during some forms of sexual activity. Such role play experiences can be powerful ways to interconnect information, feelings, and attitudes with behavior, thereby bridging between classroom learning and real life experience, while also provoking consideration of individual differences, personal values, and social controversies. An occasional practical suggestion may also be useful in helping students move from abstract knowledge to concrete behavior. For example, I may propose that the males who masturbate do so on one occasion while wearing a condom in order to compare physical sensations. Or I may recommend that the women who are sexually active purchase a spermicide and practice using it *before* they are actually in a situation in which intercourse might take place.

A SEX-POSITIVE PERSPECTIVE

As I have indicated above, sexuality education appears to be weakest in its attempts to translate sexual knowledge and attitudes/ values into applied behavior. Neither have sexuality educators fared well in meeting the challenge of a sex-positive orientation, that is, emphasizing the enhancement of sexual pleasure (both physical and emotional). Too often, a focus on hurt–the negative or threatening aspects of sexuality–has been used in an effort to convince young people to remain sexually inactive for a significant portion of their lives. Thus, teachers become agents of social control more than genuine educators–and students become understandably suspicious, or even resistant, to the learning process. Inordinate amounts of time are spent on reproductive anatomy and physiology, contraception, and STDs, compared with minimal effort affirming the pleasures of touch, the requirements for orgasmic release, or the importance of trust and open communication in specific sexual interactions.

In my college courses and presentations to other groups, I emphasize a *balance* between efforts to reduce hurt and efforts to increase pleasure. Over the years, many of my students have expressed pleasant surprise at my commitment to a sex-positive perspective. In the first session of any sexuality course, I try to convey this to the students by saying:

> I know that your motivations for taking this course are highly variable and that your experiences in expressing your sexuality are highly variable. I also know that some of you come from stable homes; some from very troubled homes. Some of you have had a good sex education; some of you have had none. Some of you have dated and been in serious relationships; some of you have not had this experience. Some of you know the pain of ending relationships. Some of you have had your first experience with sexual intercourse; some of you are committed virgins. I am not much concerned about where each of you fits within all this variation. Here is my motivation for teaching this course, and the bottom line for me: The next time you choose to give expression to your sexuality, in whatever way you choose and with whomever you choose, whether that is right after class today because it is an emergency, or tonight, or next month, or several years from now–I want that experience to be unbelievably, incredibly, fantastically, memorably, really GOOD, really PLEASURABLE! I do not want that experience to be burdened by guilt, shame, or humiliation, or by an unwanted pregnancy, an STD, feelings of coercion, or any other form of hurt. I want it to be an absolutely dynamite experience! I want you to know enough and be behaviorally prepared to avoid some of the possible hurts and to guarantee the highest level of pleasure for all involved. Remember, good

sexual experiences are not automatic. If falling in love and being married were guarantees of good sex, I would not be in my business. Learning to make sexual interaction pleasurable is as difficult as learning how to avoid getting hurt. We will try to balance our focus on both.

This message is intended to set the stage for behaviorally focused, positively oriented sexuality education. Based upon their earlier experiences, including previous sexuality education classes, some students are initially skeptical about my commitment. They are not used to being affirmed as sexual beings; much of their previous sex information has been acquired in a negative context (Kantor, 1992).

The burden is upon sexuality educators to create a positive context for learning, even when the subject matter has negative or fear-provoking elements. For example, if emphasis is placed primarily upon using condoms as an aspect of pleasurable interaction in addition to their protective potential, then students are more likely to listen and to rehearse behaviors that include condom use. Similarly, education about "safer sex" ought to include how to make safer sex more pleasurable. At appropriate times and in appropriate ways, sexuality educators need to convey details such as the fact that condoms come in various "flavors" or that condom use during oral sex can be a bridge for those persons who are initially uncomfortable with oral/genital sexual contact. In this regard, explicit films and videos can be useful for illustration.[1]

Obviously, the specifics of the behavioral component of sexuality education will vary in terms of age-appropriate objectives; however, the sex positive perspective need not vary at all. Some sort of focus on the behavioral component of sexuality is possible no matter what aspect of the curriculum is being taught at any given time. From the earliest years, sexuality education should deal directly with its behavioral implications so that it can "take hold" of the students in ways that are meaningful in their life experience, there and then. Only when it does so will sexuality education help students lay claim to their own sexuality–and responsibility for their sexual behavior–in effective and appropriate ways.

CONCLUSION

It is not surprising that the behavioral component of sexuality education and the sex-positive perspective are the most troublesome issues for educators. In my view, it is impossible to teach effectively toward the behavioral component of sexuality education without taking a sex-positive stance; conversely, to teach honestly from a sex-positive perspective demands attention to the behavioral expression of sexuality. This natural linkage between a sex-positive emphasis and explicit consideration of sexual behavior may account for the tendency of so many sexuality educators to avoid both. Perhaps the failure of sexuality education to significantly influence individual behavior is associated with the fact that it too often fails to deal with the realistic details of behavior itself? Perhaps a sex-positive perspective is the critical missing link in the translation from knowledge and attitudes/values to behavioral expression? It is my conviction that the more systemic, dialectical model of *learning by/for doing* better addresses the balance necessary for genuine understanding, making much more probably the integration of what is learned into everyday life. In other words, it is time for sexuality educators to recognize and advocate for *reversing* the widely held opinion (even by some educators themselves) that detailed discussion of sexual behavior and an emphasis on sexual pleasure will lead to irresponsible or dangerous experimentation!

If sexuality education focuses exclusively on knowledge acquisition, the result may be students who intellectualize their sexuality, students who know a great deal but do not know whether or how to act upon their sexual inclinations. If sexuality education is dominated exclusively by values clarification, the result may be students who have strong beliefs about what is right or wrong, but who have no knowledge base to practical guidelines for sexual behavior. Admittedly, to focus only upon sexual behavior would be a mistake. But to omit behavior, or to overemphasize one component of learning at the expense of the others, risks failing to meet the central goal of sexuality education: to create a context for healthy sexual expression and responsible self-fulfillment.

NOTE

1. See, for example, *Norma and Tony: Following Safer Sex Guidelines* (National Sex Forum, 1985) or *The Complete Guide to Safe Sex* (Institute for the Advanced Study of Human Sexuality, 1985).

REFERENCES

Bell, A. P. & Weinberg, M. S. (1978). *Homosexualities*. New York: Simon & Schuster.

Dailey, D. M. (1975a). Adjustment of heterosexual and homosexual couples in pairing relationships: An exploratory study. *Journal of Sex Research, 15*(2), 143-157.

Dailey, D. M. (1975b). A learning paradigm for the teaching of research in social practice. *Journal of Education for Social Work, 11*(2), 25-31.

Gordon, W. E. & Schutz, M. L. (1969). *Field Instruction Research Report*. St. Louis: George Warren Brown School of Social Work, Washington University.

Greenspan, A. & Castro, K. G. (1990). Heterosexual transmission of HIV infection. *SIECUS Report, 19*(1), 108.

Kantor, L. M. (1992). Scared chaste? Fear based educational curricula. *SIECUS Report, 21*(2), 1-15.

Kirby, D. (1984). *Sexuality Education: An Evaluation of Programs and Their Effects*. Santa Cruz, CA: Network Publications.

Kirby, D. (1985). The effects of selected sexuality education programs: Towards a more realistic view. *Journal of Sex Education and Therapy, 11*(1), 28-37.

Krueger, M. M. (1991). The omnipresent need: Professional training for sexuality education teachers. *SIECUS Report, 19*(4), 1-5.

Reed, D. A. & Munson, M. E. (1976). Resolution of one's sexual self: An important step for sexuality educators. *SIECUS Report, 17*(6), 1-6.

Ross, M. A. & Kantor, L. M. (1995). Trends in opposition to comprehensive sexuality education in public schools 1994-1995 school year. *SIECUS Report, 23*(6), 9-15.

Sagier, M. T. & Robins, E. (1973). *Male and Female Homosexuality: A Comprehensive Investigation*. Baltimore: Williams and Wilkins.

Evaluating the Effectiveness of Workshop Interventions on Contraceptive Use Among First-Year College Students

Sandra L. Caron, PhD
D. Bruce Carter, PhD
Clive M. Davis, PhD
Eleanor Macklin, PhD

SUMMARY. This study investigated the impact of interventions designed to affect contraceptive knowledge and attitudes on the intent to use and reported use of contraceptives among 362 first year college students. After completing a pretest questionnaire, students were randomly assigned to a nonintervention control group or one of four workshops utilizing different approaches to education about sexuality and contraceptive use. The posttest results indicated that all four treatment groups increased in contraceptive knowledge relative to the control group. In addition, groups receiving an experientially oriented intervention showed significantly more positive changes in their

Sandra L. Caron is affiliated with the Department of Human Development at the University of Maine. D. Bruce Carter and Clive M. Davis are affiliated with the Department of Psychology at Syracuse University. Eleanor Macklin is affiliated with the Marriage and Family Therapy Program at Syracuse University.

Address correspondence to Sandra L. Caron, PhD, Department of Human Development, University of Maine, 5749 Merrill Hall, Room 12, Orono, ME 04469-5749.

[Haworth co-indexing entry note]: "Evaluating the Effectiveness of Workshop Interventions on Contraceptive Use Among First-Year College Students." Caron, Sandra L. et al. Co-published simultaneously in *Journal of Psychology & Human Sexuality* (The Haworth Press, Inc.) Vol. 9, No. 3/4, 1997, pp. 99-120; and: *Sexuality Education in Postsecondary and Professional Training Settings* (ed: James W. Maddock) The Haworth Press, Inc., 1997, pp. 99-120. Single or multiple copies of this article are available for a fee from The Haworth Document Delivery Service [1-800-342-9678, 9:00 a.m. - 5:00 p.m. (EST). E-mail address: getinfo@haworth.com].

contraceptive attitudes than did students in the control group. More-over, students who participated in interventions focusing on experi-ential factors were significantly more likely than other students to in-dicate intent to use and reported use of birth control at the three month posttest. The overall pattern of findings support major theoreti-cal models proposed by Byrne (1977) and Fishbein (1972) of the relationships between contraceptive attitudes and use. Suggestions are made for applying these findings in sexuality education. *[Article copies available for a fee from The Haworth Document Delivery Service: 1-800-342-9678. E-mail address: getinfo@haworth.com]*

American teenagers are now engaging in premarital intercourse in greater numbers and at an earlier age than at any time in modern history (National Center for Health Statistics, 1990; Selverstone, 1989). More than a decade ago, Zelnik and Kantner (1980) reported that by the age of 19 more than two-thirds of unmarried American women and about 80% of unmarried American men had engaged in sexual intercourse at least once. Although some researchers suggest a leveling off during the 1980s of the 1970s trend reported by Zelnik and Kantner, it remains clear that the overwhelming majority of both young men and women experience sexual intercourse dur-ing their teens while unmarried (Henshaw, 1994).

Most of those engaging in sexual intercourse do not use any form of contraception for protection from pregnancy or STDs the first time they engage in sexual intercourse and, even among college students, fewer than half use contraception consistently (e.g., DeLa-mater & MacCorquodale, 1979; Hatcher & Hughes, 1988; Soren-sen, 1973). Although adolescent females constitute only 18% of sexually active American women capable of conceiving, they now account for almost 50% of all out-of-wedlock pregnancies and 25% of abortions (Henshaw & Van Vort, 1989). Moreover, while there has been an increase in the consistency of contraceptive use, nearly two-thirds of sexually active teenage girls continue to report they either never use contraception or use it erratically (Morrison, 1985). Such inconsistency in contraceptive use may account, in part, for the more than a million unplanned teenage pregnancies which occur each year (Alan Guttmacher Institute, 1989). In view of these statis-tics, it is apparent that there is an urgent need to explore the factors that influence adolescent contraceptive behavior.

Lack of information about sex and contraception has been the most commonly reported reason for lack of contraception use (e.g., Goldsmith, Gabrielson, Gabrielson, Matthews & Potts, 1972; Zelnik & Kantner, 1979). However, inadequate knowledge does not explain why many teenagers who understand the mechanics and risks of conception still do not use contraceptives or use them inconsistently. Attempts have been made to correlate contraceptive behavior with a variety of personality characteristics, but few relationships have been found (Davidson & Jaccard, 1975; Oskamp & Mindick, 1983). However, contraceptive behavior has successfully been predicted by specific psychological variables. In particular, Byrne and his colleagues (Byrne, Jazwinski, DeNinno & Fisher, 1977; Fisher, Byrne & White, 1983) have developed a model to predict contraceptive use and related attitudes on the basis of affective response to sexuality. Moreover, Fishbein and his colleagues (Ajzen & Fishbein, 1980; Davidson & Jaccard, 1975; Fishbein & Ajzen, 1975) developed a model to predict intentions to contracept and actual use based on one's specific attitudes and beliefs regarding contraception.

AFFECTIVE RESPONSE TO SEXUALITY

According to Byrne and his colleagues (Byrne & Clore, 1970; Byrne, Jazwinski, DeNinno & Fisher, 1977), effective contraceptive behaviors are mediated by affective responses to one's own sexuality. They propose that affective and evaluative responses to sexuality determine whether an individual will use contraception. These emotional responses to sexuality can be classified on a continuum from erotophobic (primarily negative attitudes regarding sexuality) to erotophilic (primarily positive attitudes toward sexuality). Using the Sexual Opinion Survey to measure erotophobic-erotophilic tendencies, Byrne and his colleagues have found that individuals with a negative affective orientation to sexuality ("erotophobic") tend not to use contraception. Subjects who responded to erotic stimuli with the most negative affect tended to have the most children, thus supporting the assumption that erotophobic orientation to sexuality may interfere with effective contraceptive behavior (Byrne, Jazwinski, DeNinno & Fisher, 1977). Several investigations have provided supportive data for this model (e.g., Fisher et al., 1979; White, Fisher, Byrne & Kingma, 1977).

Byrne proposes that an individual's beliefs, attitudes, and feelings affect behavior. He (1983) suggests that the effective use of contraception is an active process, entailing five steps requiring a series of approach-type behaviors, whereas contraceptive nonuse involves failure to perform these behaviors as well as engagement in avoidance-type behaviors. This model asserts that, in addition to the possession of accurate information (Step 1), appropriate contraceptive preparation necessitates being aware and admitting that one may have intercourse (Step 2); taking measures to acquire necessary contraceptives publicly, such as seeking medical assistance and/or purchasing contraceptives (Step 3); communicating with one's sexual partner about the use of contraceptives (Step 4); and using consistent and often complex regimens in order to avoid pregnancy (Step 5).

Research supports both the conclusion that emotional response to sexuality affects contraceptive use and the assumptions underlying the model presented above. Persons with a negative emotional response to sexuality tend to have difficulty learning what they need to know about conception and contraception necessary for Step 1 (Yarber & McCabe, 1981). Findings also indicate that erotophobic young people may not accurately anticipate future intercourse (Step 2), thus neglecting to take necessary contraceptive precautions (Fisher, 1978). Moreover, the erotophobic individuals that Fisher, Fisher and Byrne (1977) studied seemed to be reluctant to engage in public behaviors to acquire contraception (Step 3). These people also appear to find discussion of sexual topics aversive (Step 4), and to hold relatively negative attitudes about birth control (Fisher, Miller, Byrne & White, 1980). In addition, Fisher and his colleagues (Fisher et al., 1979) found erotophobic young men and women to be inconsistent users of contraception (Step 5).

ATTITUDES TOWARDS CONTRACEPTION

Fishbein and his colleagues (Ajzen, 1987; Ajzen & Fishbein, 1980; Davidson & Jaccard, 1975; Fishbein, 1972; Fishbein & Ajzen, 1975) propose a model for predicting general social behavior, in which an individual's behavior is seen as a function of personal intentions, mediated by personal attitudes toward the specific behavioral act (attitudes), along with the individual's perceptions of what "significant others" think about that behavior (subjective norms). The individual's attitude toward an act is theorized (e.g., Ajzen & Fishbein, 1980) to be a function of his or her beliefs about the consequences of performing that act and his or her evaluation of the consequences, linked to his or her perception of what significant others think the behavior should be (normative beliefs), weighted by that individual's desire to comply with these significant others (motivation to comply).[1] The Fishbein formulation necessitates specificity in defining behavior, the object, the situation in which the behavior was or would be carried out, and the time frame (Fishbein & Ajzen, 1975). For example, with regard to birth control this approach would ask about the intention to use (behavior) birth control (a particular object) during every act of sexual intercourse (situation) in the next three months (time frame).

Applying the Fishbein approach, Jaccard and Davidson (1972) investigated intentions to use contraceptives as a function of attitudes toward the act and subjective norms. Findings revealed that both attitudinal and normative factors influenced behavioral intentions. In another study, Davidson and Jaccard (1975) examined intentions of females to use contraceptives, to have a two-child family, and to have a child during the next two years. Using the Fishbein model to predict intentions, consistently high multiple correlations were found across socioeconomic and religious groups. In a study of 145 male undergraduates, Fisher (1978) found that those males who reported intention to use condoms every time they had intercourse were more likely to do so during the following month than those who did not intend to do so. These findings further support the assumptions of the Fishbein model and suggest the usefulness of this approach for understanding and predicting contraceptive behavior.

In addition to exploring the impact of attitudinal factors, Fisher (1978) also examined the role of affective response to sexuality. Affective response to sexuality and contraceptive attitudes were measured and actual contraceptive use was measured. The findings indicated that affective responses and contraceptive attitudes contributed independently to contraceptive behavior, thus affirming both the Byrne and the Fishbein approaches. On the basis of his findings, Fisher recommended that interventions designed to increase contraceptive use consider both affective and attitudinal factors.

This review suggests that contraceptive knowledge, affective response to sexuality, and attitudes (including beliefs and subjective norms) regarding contraception all impact on adolescents' use of contraception. The goal of this study was to investigate the effectiveness of various interventions designed to affect contraceptive knowledge, attitudes, and use among first-year college students.

HYPOTHESES

Hypotheses 1-4 relate to the evaluation of the four workshop interventions and explore the relationship between pretest and posttest scores for the various intervention groups.

Hypothesis 1: At the posttest, students who receive contraceptive information only will report a significantly greater increase in contraceptive knowledge than students who receive no information.

Hypothesis 2: At the posttest, students who receive interventions designed to affect contraceptive knowledge and attitudes will report greater contraceptive knowledge, more positive behavioral beliefs and attitudes, stronger intent to use contraception and, in the case of students who have engaged in sexual intercourse, greater reported use of contraception than students who receive the contraceptive information-only intervention.

Hypothesis 3: At the posttest, students who receive the experientially-oriented intervention will report more positive behavioral beliefs and attitudes, stronger intent to use contraception and, in the case of persons who engaged in sexual intercourse, greater reported use of contraception than students who received the cognitively-oriented intervention.

Hypothesis 4: At the posttest, students who receive the intervention which combines the cognitively-oriented and experientially-oriented components will have more positive behavioral beliefs and attitudes, stronger intent to use contraception and, in the case of persons who have engaged in sexual intercourse, more reported use of contraception than students in the cognitively-oriented intervention group or the experientially-oriented intervention group.

According to Fishbein's model (Fishbein & Ajzen, 1975), interventions designed to change a person's beliefs about contraceptive use are thought to influence their attitudes, intent and, finally, behavior. The attitudinal interventions employed in this study were designed to change behavioral beliefs about contraceptive use through a cognitively-oriented intervention, an experientially-oriented intervention, and a combination (cognitively- and experientially-oriented) intervention.

It was expected that the experientially-oriented intervention would be more effective in changing students' behavioral beliefs than would the cognitively-oriented intervention because it involves students more personally in the exercises (Hypothesis 3). Research suggests that "the closer the person is to the role, the more likely are his cognitive and motivational dispositions to be affected by the experience" (Culbertson, 1957, p. 230).

Finally, this study investigated the effectiveness of the combination workshop intervention in increasing students' behavioral beliefs (Hypothesis 4). This intervention was employed to ascertain whether or not a combination of the cognitively-oriented intervention and the experientially-oriented intervention would be the most effective for change.

METHOD

Procedure

Data were collected through the use of questionnaires administered by the respective floor Resident Advisors in two different sessions. The pretest was administered during a floor meeting for all hall residents during the first week of school in September to all five groups. The posttest was administered to all five groups of subjects by the Resident Assistant during the first week in December (three months after pretest) at an end-of-the-semester floor meeting for all residents. The posttest questionnaire contained the same measures as the pretest. All subjects completed an informed consent form prior to the pretest, which described the procedures of the research. At the conclusion of the posttest questionnaire, all subjects received an explanatory debriefing.

Subjects

Subjects were first-year college students living in coed residence halls at Syracuse University. Of the ten coed residence halls on campus, two were randomly selected for study. Each hall had eight floors with about seventy students per floor. Out of a total of sixteen floors, ten were selected and randomly assigned to one of the five groups. From these 726 first-year students, 426 completed the pretest questionnaire and 468 students completed the posttest questionnaire. Of the 586 students assigned to one of the four intervention groups, 257 (44%) participated. Only first-year students who completed both pre- and posttest questionnaires and the intervention, if assigned, were included in the study. Thus, of the 726 eligible students, 362 (50%) were in the final sample: 185 women (51%) and 177 men (49%). Most were 18 years of age (93%) and white (91%).

Measures

The questionnaire consisted of:

(1) Face Sheet: The face sheet contained demographic questions regarding gender, age, race, religion, and major.

(2) Sexual Behavior Survey: This is an eight-item survey of the respondent's sexual experience and use of contraceptives in the past three months, adapted from items developed by Fisher (1978). Items assessed whether they had engaged in sexual intercourse, age of first intercourse, number of times they had used birth control, type of birth control used, and number of sexual partners.

(3) Contraceptive Knowledge Scale: This scale, developed by the first author, consists of ten True/False items. Possible scores range from 0-10, with a higher score indicating greater knowledge of contraception. Items were designed to measure contraceptive information discussed during the workshop interventions. Internal consistency coefficients ranged from .24 to .46 (m = .32) for pretest, and from .26 to .47 (m = .39) for posttest. The test-retest reliability coefficient was .89.

(4) Sexual Opinion Survey: This twenty-one item scale was designed by Byrne (1983) to measure affective response to a variety of sexual situations and activities. Each item is answered on a seven-point Likert scale from "Strongly Agree" to "Strongly Disagree." Possible scores range from 0 (most erotophobic) to 126 (most erotophilic). Internal consistency coefficients ranged from .11 to .71 (m = .44) for pretest, and from .12 to .65 (m = .46) for posttest. The test-retest reliability coefficient was .98. Split-half reliabilities of .84 and above have been reported (Fisher, Byrne & White, 1983).

(5) Contraceptive Attitudes Survey: This is a forty-item survey designed to assess attitudes about contraceptive use, behavioral beliefs about contraceptive use, norms about contraceptive use, normative beliefs about contraceptive use, and intent to use contraception during intercourse in the next three months. The survey was constructed by the first author in accord with procedures outlined by Ajzen and Fishbein (1980). Internal consistency coefficients for the attitudes about contraceptive use measure ranged from .65 to .83 (m = .75) for pretest, and from .65 to .83 (m = .77) for posttest. The test-retest reliability coefficient was .89. Internal consistency coefficients for the behavioral beliefs about contraceptive use measure ranged from .08 to .68 (m = .43) for pretest, and from .01 to .78 (m = .44) for posttest. The test-retest reliability coefficient was .88. The test-retest coefficient for the one-item subjective norm measure was .81. Internal consistency coefficients for the normative beliefs about contraceptive use measure ranged from .73 to .86 (m = .79) for pretest, and from .77 to .88 (m = .82) for posttest. The test-retest reliability coefficient was .95. The test-retest reliability coefficient for the one-item intent to use contraception measure was .92.

(6) Contraceptive Process Scale: A fifteen-item scale was constructed by the first author to assess an individual's attitude toward the five steps in the contraceptive process outlined by Byrne (1983). Ten of the items were included in the Contraceptive Attitudes Survey, and five were in the Sexual Opinion Survey. For each step, participants were asked to rate their perceptions of the likelihood (likely-unlikely), desirability (good-bad), and degree of comfort (comfortable-uncomfortable). Items were rated using the bipolar adjectives separated by a seven-point scale, with total possible scores

ranging from 15 to 105. Higher scores on this measure indicated more positive responses to the contraceptive process. Internal consistency coefficients ranged from .47 to .64 (m = .56) for pretest, and from .59 to .77 (m = .65) for posttest. The test-retest coefficient was .97.

INTERVENTIONS

In addition to completing the pre- and posttest questionnaire, participants in groups 1-4 participated in 90-minute workshops conducted by the first author, designed to influence specific knowledge about and/or attitudes towards contraceptive use. Specific details of each workshop intervention outlined below are available from the first author. Since the time requirements for presentation of material in each workshop differed, it was necessary for some groups to engage in non-contraceptive discussions.

Group #1 (N = 79): Contraceptive Information-Only. Participants received information on the following methods of birth control: oral contraceptives, IUDs, diaphragms, condoms, spermicides, fertility awareness, abstinence, and sterilization. Information on unreliable methods was also provided. Some of the birth control methods were displayed (i.e., birth control pills, IUD, diaphragm, condoms, and spermicides). This presentation required thirty minutes to complete. An additional hour was spent on non-contraceptive discussion about various student organizations and activities available to new students on campus.

Group #2 (N = 76): Contraceptive Information Plus Cognitively-Oriented Intervention. In addition to providing the contraceptive information given in Group #1, this workshop included a cognitively-oriented intervention. First, students formed pairs to brainstorm the actions involved in the contraceptive process. These ideas were then shared with the entire group. The group leader then outlined the five steps of the contraceptive process identified by Byrne (1983) and facilitated a detailed discussion of each step. Following this discussion, students were divided into two groups and instructed to develop a list of popular anti-contraception and pro-contraception beliefs. These were then discussed as a group. This intervention required a total of one hour to complete. An additional thirty minutes was spent on non-contraceptive discussion about student groups and activities available on campus.

Group #3 (N = 73): Contraceptive Information Plus Experientially-Oriented Intervention. Following the thirty-minute presentation on contraceptive information, participants were led in a guided fantasy designed to "walk them through" Byrne's five steps in the contraceptive process. First, participants were instructed to find a space to lie on the floor, close their eyes, and begin to relax. After some general instructions regarding breathing and relaxation, they were told to imagine in detail attending a class on human sexuality in which they received—and retained—information on sexual activity and contraception, including viewing in their imagination a sexually explicit film involving the use of birth control. They were then instructed to imagine themselves reflecting back on the class, talking to others (including family members) about the class, imagining another individual with whom they would like to be sexual, and planning for sexual activity—including the use of contraception. Subsequently, the group leader led participants through a detailed fantasy about thoughts and actions required to obtain contraceptives, discuss their use with the imagined partner, and then actually utilize birth control in a sexual encounter. Following this extended fantasy, participants were "debriefed" by choosing another individual in the group with whom to discuss their thoughts and feelings about the exercise, after which a large group discussion on students' beliefs regarding contraception (both pro and con) took place. An additional thirty minutes was spent on non-contraceptive discussion about the various student groups and activities available on campus.

Group #4 (N = 77): Combined Group - Contraceptive Information Plus Cognitively-Oriented and Experientially-Oriented Intervention. In addition to the contraceptive information given in Group #1, participants received both the cognitively-oriented intervention (which consisted of a discussion of the five steps to contraceptive use and a discussion of popular anti-contraception and pro-contraception beliefs) and the experientially-oriented intervention (which consisted of a guided fantasy that "walked" students through the five steps of the contraceptive process and a group discussion of their personal beliefs about contraception). This workshop required a total of ninety minutes to complete.

Group #5 (N = 57): Control Group. Persons in the control group took both the pretest and posttest, but did not participate in an intervention group.

RESULTS

Responses to the Sexual Behavior Survey are presented in Table 1. Results from the pretest and posttest revealed that the majority of students (78% and 84%, respectively) had engaged in sexual intercourse. Fifty-six percent of students indicated they had experienced sexual intercourse for the first time during high school. Of those who were sexually active, the majority of students (64% pretest, 71% posttest) indicated that they had engaged in sexual intercourse within the previous three months. However, on the pretest, only 37% indicated they had used birth control every time, while on the posttest, 66% indicated that they had done so. For both pretest and posttest results, the majority of sexually active students indicated that they had had one sexual partner in the previous three months. Condoms were listed as the most common form of birth control, followed by oral contraceptives. All students were asked where they obtained information on birth control. Results were similar for both the pretest and posttest, with friends listed as the most accessible source of birth control information.

The hypotheses evaluated the effectiveness of the four major intervention strategies on students' levels of contraceptive knowledge, contraceptive attitudes, intent to use contraceptives, and reported use of contraceptives. Difference scores were computed for each dependent variable of interest by subtracting the pretest score on that variable from the posttest score. A multivariate analysis of variance (MANOVA) was then computed on these difference scores. High scores indicate greater contraceptive knowledge, more positive attitudes, greater intent to use contraceptives, or greater reported use of contraceptives.

The sample size for analyses of all students completing both the pretest and posttest measures was 362. Since not all students had engaged in sexual intercourse in the three months preceding the pretest and the three months preceding the posttest, the sample size for analysis of reported use of contraceptives was 200.

TABLE 1. Sexual behavior information for all subjects (pre- and posttest).

Have you ever had sexual intercourse? (N = 362)

	Yes	No
Pretest	78%	22%
Posttest	84%	16%

Age of first intercourse (N = 362)

	≤15	15-17	18-19	N/A
Pretest	11%	56%	11%	22%
Posttest	11%	56%	17%	16%

Sexual activity in past three months

	Yes	No
Pretest (N = 233)	64%	36%
Posttest (N = 257)	71%	29%

If sexually active, did you use birth control every time?

	Yes	No
Pretest (N = 233)	37%	63%
Posttest (N = 257)	66%	34%

Number of partners in the past three months

	1	2	3-4	5-6	7-8	9>
Pretest (N = 233)	62%	26%	11%	1%	0	0
Posttest (N = 257)	67%	17%	12%	2%	0	2%

Method(s) of Birth Control

	Condom	Pill	Diaph.	Sp'cides	NFP	IUD	Other
Pretest (N = 233)	62%	25%	6%	6%	5%	1%	2%
Posttest (N = 257)	65%	29%	8%	14%	2%	0	0

Sources of Birth Control Information (N = 362)

	Friends	Class	Reading	Doctor/Clinic	Family
Pretest	73%	56%	40%	31%	26%
Posttest	85%	61%	48%	32%	27%

	Partner	Church	Other
Pretest	22%	13%	4%
Posttest	26%	14%	5%

Multivariate Analyses of Variance

Examination of the results of a 2 (gender of student) × 5 (control group and the four intervention groups) MANOVA using Pillai's Trace Test of Significance indicated no significant effect for gender of student, $F(5, 348) = 1.30$, n.s., nor did gender of student interact with group membership, $F(20, 1404) = 1.15$, n.s. There was, however, a significant multivariate effect for workshop intervention membership, $F(20, 1404) = 13.33$, $p < .0001$. Results of univariate tests of the main effects of group membership on each of the dependent variables were then examined.

Mean difference scores (pretest-posttest) for students in each of the groups are presented in Table 2. Univariate analyses of variance indicated significant group differences on knowledge $F(4, 352) = 36.67$, $p < .0001$, behavioral beliefs about contraceptive use $F(4,$

TABLE 2. Mean difference scores (posttest-pretest) for students in each treatment group for scores on contraceptive knowledge, behavioral beliefs, attitudes about contraceptive use, attitudes about the contraceptive process, intent to use contraception and reported use of contraception.[1]

Group: Multivariate $F(20, 1404) = 13.33$, $p < .0001$

	Contraceptive Knowledge	Behavioral Beliefs	Attitudes About BC Use	Attitudes About Process	Intent to Use Birth Control	Use of Birth Control[2]
	(N = 362)	(N = 362)	(N = 362)	(N = 362)	(N = 362)	(N = 200)
CONTROL	0.42[c]	−3.40[a]	1.00[b]	0.54[d]	0.09[b]	−3[c]
N = 57/34						
INFO	3.00[a]	0.34[a]	1.33[ab]	9.62[b]	0.27[b]	10[bc]
N = 79/56						
COG	2.42[b]	1.93[a]	0.71[b]	6.65[c]	0.04[b]	26[ab]
N = 76/41						
EXPER	2.45[b]	−10.95[b]	1.89[a]	16.04[a]	0.84[a]	37[a]
N = 73/34						
COMBO	2.73[ab]	−15.36[b]	2.12[a]	16.83[a]	0.68[a]	23[ab]
N = 77/39						
$F(4, 352) =$	36.67	10.18	4.22	44.04	6.42	4.34
	$p < .0001$	$p < .0001$	$p < .005$	$p < .0001$	$p < .0001$	$p < .005$

[1] Means within a column with differing superscripts are significantly different ($p < .05$) from one another based on results from the Duncan Multiple Range Test (Kirk, 1968).
[2] Scores on use of birth control are changes in percentage of times birth control was reportedly used.

352) = 10.18, $p < .0001$, attitudes toward contraceptive use $F(4, 352) = 4.22$, $p < .005$, attitudes toward the contraceptive process $F(4, 352) = 44.04$, $p < .0001$, and intent to use birth control $F(4, 352) = 6.42$, $p < .005$ scores. Examination of the means presented in Table 2 and results of the Duncan Multiple Range Test (Kirk, 1968; $p < .05$) indicated the following patterns of differences:

Contraceptive Knowledge Scores. Students in all intervention groups showed significantly greater increases in contraceptive knowledge than did students in the control group. Students in the information-only group showed significantly greater increases in contraceptive knowledge than did their peers in the cognitively-oriented and experientially-oriented groups. No other differences in contraceptive knowledge between groups were significant. Thus, simply receiving contraceptive information had the effect of raising students' knowledge scores.

Behavioral Beliefs About Contraceptive Use. Students in the control, information-only, and cognitively-oriented groups showed significantly greater increases in behavioral beliefs about contraceptive use than did students in the experientially-oriented and combination groups. Thus, the two groups containing the experientially-oriented interventions did not appear to be as effective in changing students' behavioral beliefs about the use of contraceptives as the nonexperientially-oriented interventions.

Attitudes Toward Contraceptive Use. Students in the experientially-oriented and combination groups showed significantly greater increases in positive attitudes about contraceptive use than did students in the control, information-only, and cognitively-oriented groups. Thus, those groups that incorporated an experiential component appeared more effective in changing students' attitudes about the use of contraceptives.

Attitudes Toward the Contraceptive Process. Students in all treatment groups showed significantly greater increases in positive attitudes toward the contraceptive process than did students in the control group. Students in the experientially-oriented and combination groups showed significantly greater increases in such attitudes than did students in the control, information-only, and cognitively-oriented groups. The information-only group showed significantly greater increase in positive attitudes than the cognitively-oriented group, but not as great as the experientially-oriented and combination groups. Overall, the greatest increase in students' positive attitudes toward the contraceptive process appeared in groups with the experientially-oriented component.

Intent to Use Birth Control. Students in the experientially-oriented and combination groups showed significantly greater increase in intention to use birth control than did students in the control, information-only and cognitively-oriented groups. No significant differences in students' intent to use birth control scores were found among the control, information-only and cognitively-oriented groups. Thus, the groups containing the experientially-oriented intervention component appeared most effective in increasing students' intent to use contraceptives.

Use of Birth Control. Only the 200 students who reported having engaged in sexual intercourse across this six-month period could be included in analyses focusing on reported use of contraceptives. Thus, a separate analysis of variance was computed for these scores. Inspection of the results of a 2 (gender of student) × 5 (group) analysis of variance indicated a significant main effect for group on use of birth control scores, $F(4, 190) = 4.34$, $p < .005$, and a significant group × gender interaction $F(4, 190) = 2.92$, $p < .05$. The effect for gender was nonsignificant.

For group differences, examination of the patterns of means and results of the Duncan Multiple Range Test (Kirk, 1968; $p < .05$) indicated that students in the cognitively-oriented, experientially-oriented, and combination treatment groups showed significantly greater increases in reported use of birth control than did their peers in the information-only and control groups. Thus, the largest increases in reported use of birth control scores appeared in groups receiving cognitive and/or experiential interventions, with the greatest increase in the experientially-oriented group.

Since there was a significant group × gender interaction, the pattern of means for males and females in the five groups were examined separately (see Table 3). The main effect for group within the male subsample was significant, $F(4, 103) = 2.92$, $p < .05$. Examination of the pattern of means indicated that students in the combination group showed significantly greater increases in reported use of birth control than did students in the control and

TABLE 3. Changes in percentage of times birth control was reportedly used by males and females in each treatment group.[1]

Group × gender: Multivariate $F(4, 190) = 2.92$, $p < .05$

Group	Males	Females
CONTROL	-1.0^b	-6.0^c
INFO	10.6^b	8.5^b
COG	23.5^{ab}	28.2^{ab}
EXPER	26.9^{ab}	55.5^a
COMBO	47.8^a	2.4^b
$F(4, 103)$	$= 2.90, p < .05$	$= 3.74, p < .05$

[1] Percentages within a column with differing superscripts are significantly different ($p < .05$) from one another based on results from the Duncan Multiple Range Test (Kirk, 1968).

information-only groups, with the cognitively-oriented and experientially-oriented groups showing important increases. It is noteworthy that while all of the male students in the intervention groups showed some increase in contraceptive use, those in the control group actually showed a *decrease* in reported use of birth control.

Examination of the main effects of group membership on changes in females' reported use of birth control also showed significant differences among groups, $F(4, 190) = 3.74, p < .05$. In this case, students in all four intervention groups showed significantly greater ($p < .05$) reported use of birth control than did students in the control group, based on results from the Duncan Multiple Range Test. Students in the experientially-oriented group scored significantly higher than their peers in the information-only and combination groups. No other significant differences emerged.

The combination intervention was the most effective treatment for males, the experientially-oriented intervention was the most effective treatment for females, although all interventions were effective in increasing females' reported use of birth control. Since both the combination and experientially-oriented treatments involve the experientially-oriented component, this component appeared to be effective for both males and females, given the overall patterns of differences.

Summary of MANOVA Findings

The pattern of results generally supported the hypotheses. Hypothesis 1 predicted that at the posttest students in the "contraceptive information-only" group would show a significantly greater increase in contraceptive knowledge than students in the control group who received no information. Inspection of this planned comparison indicated a significant difference between the information-only and control group on contraceptive knowledge scores. Further comparison of the means for contraceptive knowledge indicated that students in all groups receiving contraceptive information scored higher than their peers in the control group on contraceptive knowledge. Thus, hypothesis 1 was supported.

Hypothesis 2 stated that, at the posttest, students who received interventions expected to affect knowledge and attitudes (i.e., cognitively-oriented, experientially-oriented, and combination groups) would report greater increases in contraceptive knowledge, more positive contraceptive behavioral beliefs and positive attitudes, greater intent to use contraception, and greater use of birth control than students who received the contraceptive information-only intervention. Examination of the pattern of means for these variables indicated that, in general, the experientially-oriented and combination groups confirmed this hypothesis. For contraceptive knowledge scores, students in the information-only group reported the greatest increase in contraceptive knowledge from pretest to posttest. For behavioral beliefs about contraceptive use scores, students in the information-only and cognitively-oriented groups showed the greatest increase. Thus, hypothesis 2 was only partially supported.

Hypothesis 3 predicted that, at the posttest, students in the experientially-oriented group would report more positive contraceptive behavioral beliefs and attitudes, greater intent to use contraception, and greater reported use of birth control than students in the cognitively-oriented group. Examination of the pattern of means for students in these two groups on attitudes toward contraceptive use, attitudes toward the contraceptive process, intent and use of birth control scores supported the hypothesis. However, students' contraceptive knowledge scores for the experientially-oriented group were not significantly different from those for the cognitively-oriented group, and students in the cognitively-oriented group reported a greater increase in scores on behavioral beliefs about contraceptive use. Therefore, when compared to the cognitively-oriented intervention, the experientially-oriented intervention had a significantly greater impact on students' contraceptive attitudes, intent to use, and reported use of contraceptives, but not on their knowledge and beliefs. Thus, hypothesis 3 was partially supported.

Hypothesis 4 stated that students in the combination group would report greater increases in contraceptive behavioral belief scores, attitudes scores, intent to use birth control, and reported use of contraceptives than students in the experientially-oriented and cognitively-oriented groups. Examination of the pattern of means did not confirm this hypothesis. For behavioral belief scores, students in the cognitively-oriented group scored higher than students in either the experientially-oriented and combination group. For all other mean scores, the experientially-oriented and combination groups were virtually equivalent.

Overall, findings in this study suggest that interventions containing information about contraception are effective for increasing contraceptive knowledge. However, information about contraception clearly is not enough to assure effective contraceptive use. Additional interventions–specifically experientially-oriented interventions–are needed to positively affect students' contraceptive attitudes and to increase contraceptive intent and use.

CONCLUSIONS

As expected, students in the four intervention groups, all of which contained the contraceptive information component, showed significantly greater increases in contraceptive knowledge than did students in the nonintervention control group. The control group stayed virtually the same on contraceptive knowledge from pretest to posttest, although their knowledge might have been expected to increase due to obtaining contraceptive information from other sources.

Given the fact that the experientially-oriented component was designed to develop more positive attitudes toward contraceptives through the use of a guided fantasy, changes in attitudes on the part of students in the experiential and combination groups was predictable. More surprising is the fact that the attitudes toward contraception of the students in the cognitively-oriented intervention group did not also become significantly more positive from pretest to posttest, since this intervention also was designed to develop more positive attitudes toward contraceptives through the use of discussion.

Overall, the workshop interventions appeared to be successful in improving students' contraceptive knowledge, attitudes about contraceptive use and the contraceptive process, intention to use, and actual use of contraceptives. In particular, the interventions containing the experientially-oriented component appeared to have the greatest impact. In every case, students participating in the experientially-oriented workshops scored significantly higher on these variables than did their peers in the control group; in some cases, students in the experientially-oriented groups scored significantly higher than did students in the groups receiving the other interventions. It seems important to consider implications of these findings for the development of interventions designed to address contraceptive use.

The results of the present study clearly indicate the importance of addressing attitudinal components in contraceptive use, the need to design contraceptive education to impact on attitudes, and the positive effect of experientially-oriented interventions on changing contraceptive attitudes and behavior. Specifically, the descriptive findings alone suggest that educational programs about contraceptives should begin at the time of entry into college, preferably as part of new student orientation. Such education should include not only basic information on the various methods available, but should also focus on the other steps identified by Byrne (1983) as important to effective use of contraception, including acknowledging the likelihood of engaging in sexual intercourse, obtaining the relevant contraceptive, communicating with a partner, and using contraception consistently. Results of this study indicate that these steps will be accomplished most effectively through experientially-oriented interventions such as guided fantasy and role plays. Denial runs high in adolescents. It is likely that information alone will not significantly increase contraceptive use. Rather, educators need to address each individual's attitudes and decision-making process, speaking to both the mind and the heart.

NOTE

1. It should be noted that any individual may have several or many salient reference persons and/or groups.

REFERENCES

Ajzen, I. (1987). Attitudes, traits and actions: Dispositions prediction of behavior in personality and social psychology. *Advances in Experimental Social Psychology, 20,* 1-63.

Ajzen, I., and Fishbein, M. (1980). *Understanding attitudes and predicting behavior.* Englewood Cliffs, NJ: Prentice-Hall, Inc.

Alan Guttmacher Institute (1989). *Risk and responsibility: Teaching sex education in America's schools today.* New York: Alan Guttmacher Institute.

Byrne, D. (1977). Social psychology and the study of sexual behavior. *Personality and Social Psychology Bulletin, 1,* 3-30.

Byrne, D. (1983). Sex without contraception. In D. Byrne and W.A. Fisher (eds.), *Adolescents, sex, and contraception* (pp. 3-32). Hillsdale, NJ: Lawrence Erlbaum Associates.

Byrne, D., and Clore, G.L. (1970). A reinforcement model of evaluation responses. *Personality: An International Journal, 1,* 103-128.

Byrne, D., Jazwinski, C., DeNinno, J.A., and Fisher, W.A. (1977). Negative sexual attitudes and contraception. In D. Byrne and L.A. Byrne (eds.), *Exploring human sexuality.* New York: Harper and Row.

Culbertson, F.M. (1957). Modification of an emotionally held attitude through role playing. *Journal of Abnormal Social Psychology, 54,* 230-233.

Davidson, A.R., and Jaccard, J.J. (1975). Population psychology: A new look at an old problem. *Journal of Personality and Social Psychology, 71,* 1073-1082.

DeLamater, J., and MacCorquodale, P.C. (1979). *Premarital sexuality: Attitudes, relationships and behavior.* Madison, WI: University of Wisconsin Press.

Fishbein, M. (1972). Toward an understanding of family planning behaviors. *Journal of Applied Social Psychology, 2,* 214-227.

Fishbein, M., and Ajzen, I. (1975). *Belief, attitude, intention, and behavior: An introduction to theory and research.* Reading, MA: Addison Wesley.

Fisher, W.A. (1978). *Affective, attitudinal, and normative determinants of contraceptive behavior among university men.* Unpublished doctoral dissertation, Purdue University.

Fisher, W.A., Byrne, D., Edmunds, M., Miller, C.T., Kelly, K., and White, L.A.

(1979). Psychological and situation-specific correlates of contraceptive behavior among university women. *The Journal of Sex Research, 15,* 38-55.

Fisher, W.A., Byrne, D., and White, L.A. (1983). Emotional barriers to contraception. In D. Byrne and W.A. Fisher (eds.), *Adolescents, sex, and contraception* (pp. 207-239). Hillsdale, NJ: Lawrence Erlbaum Assoc.

Fisher, W.A., Fisher, J.D., and Byrne, D. (1977). Consumer reactions to contraceptive purchasing. *Personality and Social Psychology Bulletin, 3,* 293-296.

Fisher, W.A., Miller, C.T., Byrne, D., and White, L.A. (1980). Talking dirty: Responses to communicating a sexual message as a function of situational and personality factors. *Basic and Applied Social Psychology, 1,* 115-126.

Goldsmith, S., Gabrielson, M., Gabrielson, I., Matthews, V., and Potts, L. (1972). Sex and contraception. *Family Planning Perspectives, 4,* 32-38.

Hatcher, R.A., and Hughes, M.S. (1988). The truth about condoms. *SIECUS Report, 17*(2), 1-8.

Henshaw, S.K. (1994). *U.S. teenage pregnancy statistics.* New York: The Alan Guttmacher Institute.

Henshaw, S.K., and Van Vort, J. (1989). Teenage abortion, birth, and pregnancy statistics: An update. *Family Planning Perspectives, 21,* 85-88.

Jaccard, J.J., and Davidson, A.R. (1972). Toward an understanding of family planning behavior: An initial investigation. *Journal of Applied Social Psychology, 2,* 228-235.

Kirk, R.E. (1968). *Experimental design: Procedures for the behavioral sciences.* Belmont, CA: Brooks/Cole.

Morrison, D.M. (1985). Adolescent contraceptive behavior: A review. *Psychological Bulletin, 98,* 538-568.

National Center for Health Statistics (1990). *Vital statistics of the United States, 1988, Vol. 1, Natality,* U.S. Government Printing Office, Washington, D.C.

Oskamp, S., and Mindick, B. (1983). Personality and attitudinal barriers to contraception. In D. Byrne and W.A. Fisher (eds.), *Adolescents, sex, and contraception* (pp. 65-107). Hillsdale, NJ: Lawrence Erlbaum Associates.

Selverstone, R. (1989). Where are we now in the sexual revolution? *SIECUS Report, 17*(4), 7-12.

Sorensen, R. (1973). *Adolescent sexuality in contemporary America.* New York: World Publishing.

White, L.A., Fisher, W.A., Byrne, D., and Kingma, R. (1977). *Development and validation of a measure of affective orientation to erotic stimuli: The Sexual Opinion Survey.* Paper presented at the meeting of the Midwestern Psychological Association, Chicago.

Yarber, W.L., and McCabe, G.P. (1981). Teacher characteristics and the inclusion of sex education topics in grades 6-8 and 9-11. *Journal of School Health, 51,* 288-291.

Zelnik, M., and Kantner, J.F. (1979). Reasons for nonuse of contraception among sexually active women aged fifteen to nineteen. *Family Planning Perspectives, 11,* 289-296.

Zelnik, M., and Kantner, J.F. (1980). Sexual activity, contraceptive use, and pregnancy among metropolitan-area teenagers: 1971-1979. *Family Planning Perspectives, 12,* 230-237.

Teaching Our Teachers to Teach: A Study on Preparation for Sexuality Education and HIV/AIDS Prevention

Monica Rodriguez
Rebecca Young, MA
Stacie Renfro
Marysol Asencio, DrPH
Debra W. Haffner, MPH

SUMMARY. This report reviews the amount and type of sexuality education at a sample of 169 institutions offering undergraduate preparation of teachers. The study was based on a review of course

---

Monica Rodriguez, Stacie Renfro, and Debra W. Haffner are affiliated with the Sexuality Information and Education Council of the United States (SIECUS). Rebecca Young and Marysol Asencio are affiliated with the Division of Sociomedical Sciences at Columbia University, New York.

Address correspondence to Monica Rodriguez, SIECUS, 130 West 42nd Street, Suite 350, New York, NY 10036.

The study reported here was made possible by grant No. U87/CCU 210194 from the U.S. Centers for Disease Control and Prevention, National Center for Chronic Disease Prevention and Health Promotion, Division of Adolescent and School Health. Its contents are the sole responsibility of the authors and do not represent the official views of the U.S. Centers for Disease Control and Prevention.

[Haworth co-indexing entry note]: "Teaching Our Teachers to Teach: A Study on Preparation for Sexuality Education and HIV/AIDS Prevention." Rodriguez, Monica et al. Co-published simultaneously in *Journal of Psychology & Human Sexuality* (The Haworth Press, Inc.) Vol. 9, No. 3/4, 1997, pp. 121-141; and: *Sexuality Education in Postsecondary and Professional Training Settings* (ed: James W. Maddock) The Haworth Press, Inc., 1997, pp. 121-141. Single or multiple copies of this article are available for a fee from The Haworth Document Delivery Service [1-800-342-9678, 9:00 a.m. - 5:00 p.m. (EST). E-mail address: getinfo@haworth.com].

catalogs to allow for a systematic comparison of a sample of programs using the same criteria. Three questions are addressed: Do teacher certification programs offer courses designed to prepare preservice teachers to teach health education, sexuality educations, and HIV/AIDS prevention education? Are courses required or elective? Are sexuality education programs for preservice teachers comprehensive? Findings are summarized, and the article concludes with several recommendations for improved teacher preparation. *[Article copies available for a fee from The Haworth Document Delivery Service: 1-800-342-9678. E-mail address: getinfo@haworth.com]*

Concern about teacher training for sexuality education dates back to the beginning of the century. As early as 1912, the National Education Association called for programs to prepare teachers for sexuality education. In 1955, the National Association of Secondary School Principals reported that there seemed to be an increasing number of courses for the preparation of sexuality educators. In 1968, the permanent Joint Committee of the National School Boards Association and the American Association of School Administrators said that the implementation of sexuality education programs in the schools "places a responsibility on local school boards and state departments of education and teacher training institutions to provide qualified teachers" (Carrera, 1972). Organizations such as SIECUS have long called for improved teacher training in sexuality education.

The vast majority of those who teach sexuality education are not sexuality educators. In fact, physical education teachers account for the largest number of those providing sexuality education in middle and high schools–followed by health educators, biology teachers, home economics teachers, and school nurses (Forest and Silverman, 1989). Classroom teachers are most likely to provide health-related instruction in elementary schools (Hausman and Ruzek, 1995).

Although over three-quarters of those teaching sexuality education classes report some undergraduate training in this area, there has been no study of the content of their training (Forest and Silverman, 1989). In a recent survey of 156 inner-city elementary teachers, only 19% reported any preservice training in health education, and only one teacher had received that training within the past five years (Hausman and Ruzek, 1995).

In most studies, teachers report they do not feel adequately trained to teach HIV/AIDS prevention and sexuality education. They report concern about their ability to teach personal skills (Levenson-Gingiss and Hamilton, 1989b), about their knowledge of HIV/AIDS (particularly as it relates to having a child with AIDS in the classroom) (Ballard, White, and Glascoff, 1990), or about their knowledge of STDs (Levenson-Gingiss and Hamilton, 1989b). They also feel they need help in teaching such subjects as sexual orientation, risk behaviors that include drug use, and safer sex practices (Kerr, Allensworth, and Gayle, 1989). Most of those teaching HIV/AIDS prevention and sexuality education have received their training in short workshops or seminars (Forest and Silverman, 1989).

Although the vast majority of states require or recommend teaching about sexuality or HIV/AIDS, only 12 states, the District of Columbia, and Puerto Rico require any certification for teachers of sexuality education, and only 12 states and the District of Columbia require certification for teachers of HIV/AIDS prevention education. Only six states and Puerto Rico require teacher training for sexuality educators; nine states, the District of Columbia, and Puerto Rico require training for teachers of HIV/AIDS prevention education (SIECUS, 1995).

If HIV/AIDS prevention and sexuality education programs are to prove effective, teachers must be prepared to teach these subjects. The best way to train teachers initially is through preservice training. Given the large numbers of teachers with undergraduate training who teach sexuality and health education, undergraduate teacher training programs need to be evaluated for their existing curricula on comprehensive sexuality education. This preservice professional training will become the foundation upon which to base effective HIV/AIDS prevention and sexuality education curricula in schools.

METHODOLOGY

This study addressed three questions about preservice teacher preparation: (1) Do teacher certification programs offer courses designed to prepare preservice teachers to teach health education, sexuality education, and HIV/AIDS prevention education? (2) Are such courses required or elective? (3) Are sexuality education programs for preservice teachers comprehensive?

Sample

We used a two-stage, systematic sampling strategy to select institutions for this study. First, we selected every fourth institution in the Membership Directory of the American Association of Colleges for Teacher Education (AACTE).[1] Next, we selected the first institution in each state listing (or the next one if the first was already selected). Four states and territories had only one school listed; therefore, they contributed no new institutions to the sample in the second stage. This sampling process resulted in 231 institutions selected for the study.

We requested undergraduate course catalogs from the 231 institutions. Six were eliminated as ineligible because they did not offer undergraduate teacher training. From the remaining 225, a total of 169 usable catalogs were received. An additional 28 institutions replied, but they did not provide sufficient information about courses for inclusion in the survey. In general, these schools only sent letters. There was no response from the remaining 28 schools. The final response rate for complete, eligible surveys was 75%. All catalogs covered the 1993, 1994, or 1995 school years. Therefore, the final analysis was based on a sample of 169 institutions offering undergraduate teacher preparation in the United States that appear representative of AACTE member institutions.

Criteria for Including Courses

Based on the title and description, courses were selected if they were:

- available to students pursuing undergraduate teacher preparation (required, recommended, and elective courses), *and*
- the main focus of the course could be classified as either health education or human sexuality, *or*
- the main focus of the course was a sexuality-related key concept delineated by the SIECUS *Guidelines for Comprehensive Sexuality Education: Kindergarten–12th Grade.*

We abstracted 819 courses offered by the following departments: teacher education, health education, physical education, psychology, sociology, biology, religion, women's studies, human development and family studies, and home economics. All courses were chosen because they had the potential to cover sexuality issues based on course titles and descriptions. The sample included both general issues and methodology courses. Health education courses with a broad focus were abstracted and were classified as health education courses (n = 434). Health courses with a very specific focus that was not sexuality-related (such as nutrition or first aid) were not included in the sample. Those that specifically mentioned one or more key concepts as a focus of the course were classified as human sexuality courses (n = 385). (See Table 1.)

Survey Instrument

Using the SIECUS *Guidelines for Comprehensive Sexuality Education: Kindergarten–12th Grade,* we developed a survey instrument to obtain information from the catalogs. This instrument gathered information on course content as well as general institutional characteristics, such as type of institution, location, student population, and teacher certification programs offered. Two general course

TABLE 1. Focus of Course by Number of Courses Offered and Required

FOCUS OF COURSE	NUMBER OF COURSES OFFERED AT ALL SCHOOLS	PERCENT OF COURSES REQUIRED FOR AT LEAST ONE CERTIFICATION PROGRAM
GENERAL HEALTH EDUCATION	434	81% (n = 350)
HUMAN SEXUALITY	385	16% (n = 60)
HIV/AIDS ISSUES	24	33% (n = 8)

categories were selected: health education and sexuality, since they were most likely to include sexuality-related components.

Content Analysis

Each program was reviewed in two ways to determine if it included the six key concepts and topics identified in the *Guidelines*. First, the number of key concepts listed in the course description was totaled and then used to determine the degree of comprehensiveness of any single sexuality-related course. Second, the number of different concepts presented across all of the school's abstracted courses was added. This number was interpreted as the comprehensiveness of the institution's entire sexuality education curriculum for teachers.

Course titles were also analyzed to gauge the overall focus of the course and to provide a second method for evaluating the sexuality education that teachers in training are offered. Since this content analysis is not as dependent on the level of detail in the catalogs, it provides some validation of the findings based on course descriptions.

Data Analysis

The abstracted surveys were coded, scanned (using the *Teleform 3.1* program), and entered into *SPSS-PC+* (a social science statistical computer package) for analysis. Course titles were also analyzed qualitatively, using content analysis techniques for grouping themes and key words.

Limitations

The use of catalogs to evaluate teacher training programs has limitations. The information abstracted for each course is based solely on the description listed in the catalog. It may not include all of the topics covered in a specific course and does not include a syllabus, underlying philosophy, required readings, instructor background, and instructor emphasis. We did not have data available on how many students actually take these courses, or on how well they perform when they do take them.

Because this analysis was based solely on information abstracted from course descriptions and titles in institutional catalogs, the content analysis inevitably reflects the level of detail in the catalog as well as the breadth of the courses reviewed. Some courses may actually cover more of the key concepts than appear in their descriptions. Others may be listed but not offered during every academic year. Required courses are more likely available annually while elective courses are often taught on a rotating basis. Some schools list courses even though they are taught only every two to three years.

Thus, while the analysis is probably a conservative estimate of the comprehensiveness of sexuality education in undergraduate training, the overall analysis probably overstates the number of available sexuality-related courses.

RESULTS

Institutional Characteristics

This sample of 169 colleges and universities that prepare preservice teachers is composed of 52% public, 5% private secular, and 43% private religious colleges and universities in the United States. Half (50%) have student populations of 3,000 or less; 7% have a student population greater than 15,000.

Almost all the colleges and universities offering teacher preparation programs offer certification in elementary (98%) and secondary education (98%). Many also offer certification in physical education (64%), health education (41%), and joint physical/health education (12%). Only 2% offer family life education certification programs. These are offered through their home economics departments. None of the required course descriptions in the family life education certification programs explicitly mention topics related to sexual health, sexual behavior, or personal skills. In addition, 6% of the institutions offer other teaching certification programs that have some sexuality or HIV/AIDS course requirements. The other majors represented in this category are home economics, special education, and child development and family studies. (See Table 2.)

Courses in Health, Sexuality, and HIV/AIDS

Almost all of the institutions offer at least one class to preservice teachers in general health education (87%) or human sexuality

TABLE 2. Percentage of Schools Offering Certification by Certification Program (N = 169)

CERTIFICATION PROGRAM	PERCENTAGE OF SCHOOLS OFFERING CERTIFICATION
ELEMENTARY EDUCATION	98% (n = 166)
SECONDARY EDUCATION	98% (n = 165)
PHYSICAL EDUCATION	64% (n = 108)
HEALTH EDUCATION	41% (n = 69)
HEALTH AND PHYSICAL EDUCATION COMBINED	12% (n = 20)
FAMILY LIFE EDUCATION	2% (n = 3)
OTHER TEACHER CERTIFICATION PROGRAMS*	6% (n = 10)

*These certification programs contain some sexuality education coursework. The certification programs represented are home economics, special education, and child development programs.

(94%). However, most do not offer classes that cover HIV/AIDS (only 12% offer courses that mention HIV/AIDS in their course descriptions). (See Table 3.) And only 9% of the general health education course descriptions contain specific language related to sexuality or HIV/AIDS. In general, sexuality is mentioned as one topic among others, such as mental health, stress reduction, substance abuse, disease prevention, and nutrition.

Many of the institutions offer several general health education courses (excluding first aid, nutrition, and other topics not directly relevant to human sexuality): 56% offer one to three courses; 24%, four to five courses; and 6%, six or more courses. Many also offer

TABLE 3. Focus of Course by Percentage of Schools Offering or Requiring Coursework (N = 169)

FOCUS OF COURSE	PERCENT OF SCHOOLS OFFERING AT LEAST ONE COURSE	PERCENT OF SCHOOLS REQUIRING AT LEAST ONE COURSE FOR AT LEAST ONE CERTIFICATION PROGRAM	PERCENT OF SCHOOLS REQUIRING AT LEAST ONE COURSE FOR ALL CERTIFICATION PROGRAMS
GENERAL HEALTH EDUCATION*	87% (n = 147)	79% (n = 133)	14% (n = 23)
HUMAN SEXUALITY	94% (n = 159)	33% (n = 56)	0
HIV/AIDS ISSUES	12% (n = 21)	4% (n = 7)	0

*These figures exclude courses in first aid, nutrition, and other specific topics not relevant to human sexuality.

several sexuality courses: 74% offer one to three courses and 20% offer four to five courses. One school offers seven courses. Only 11% of the schools offered one course covering HIV/AIDS, and three schools offered two courses. (See Table 4.)

This study also looked at how many courses are designed to help preservice teachers learn the pedagogy and methodology of health education, sexuality education, and HIV/AIDS prevention education. Most schools (72%) offer classes in health education methods. However, few schools (12%) offer methods courses in sexuality education. Only 4% offer courses that include methods training in HIV/AIDS prevention education. (See Table 5.)

Course Requirements in Health, Sexuality, and HIV/AIDS

One way to measure whether preservice teachers will receive training in a certain area is to examine required courses. Most schools (79%) require at least one general health education course for at least one certification program, and many (33%) require at

274

TABLE 4. Number of Courses Offered by Schools in the Areas of Health, Sexuality, and HIV/AIDS (N = 169)

NUMBER OF COURSES	HEALTH EDUCATION COURSES*	SEXUALITY COURSES	HIV/AIDS ISSUES COURSES
0	13% (n = 22)	6% (n = 10)	88% (n = 148)
1	22% (n = 38)	30% (n = 50)	11% (n = 18)
2-3	34% (n = 58)	44% (n = 75)	2% (n = 3)
4-5	24% (n = 41)	20% (n = 33)	0
6-9	6% (n = 10)	1% (n = 1)	0

*These figures exclude courses in first aid, nutrition, and other specific topics not relevant to human sexuality.

least one sexuality course for at least one certification program. (See Table 3.) Hardly any (4%) require courses covering HIV/AIDS for any programs. Of all abstracted courses, 81% of the health education courses, 16% of the sexuality courses, and 33% of the courses covering HIV/AIDS are required for at least one certification program. (See Table 1.)

Only 14% of the surveyed schools require a health education course for all preservice teachers. (See Table 3.) None require courses covering HIV/AIDS or sexuality for all preservice teachers, although one does recommend sexuality courses for all teacher certification programs. Almost three-quarters (72%) of the schools offer courses in the pedagogy and methodology of health education for their preservice teachers. Twelve percent of schools offer a course in the pedagogy and methodology of sexuality education. Only 4% of schools offer methodology courses which include HIV/AIDS prevention education for any teacher certification program.

Most schools in the sample (63%) require a course in health education teaching methods for at least one preservice certification program. Only three (2%) require a methods course for all preservice certification programs. Less than one in ten of the schools (8%) require sexuality education teaching methods courses for any certi-

TABLE 5. Percentage of Schools Offering and Requiring Teaching Methods Courses (N = 169)

FOCUS OF METHODS COURSE	PERCENT OF SCHOOLS OFFERING AT LEAST ONE COURSE	PERCENT OF SCHOOLS REQUIRING AT LEAST ONE METHODS COURSE FOR AT LEAST ONE CERTIFICATION PROGRAM	PERCENT OF SCHOOLS REQUIRING AT LEAST ONE METHODS COURSE FOR ALL CERTIFICATION PROGRAMS
GENERAL HEALTH EDUCATION METHODS	72% (n = 121)	63% (n = 106)	2% (n = 3)
SEXUALITY EDUCATION METHODS	12% (n = 20)	8% (n = 13)	0
HIV/AIDS PREVENTION EDUCATION METHODS	4% (n = 6)	4% (n = 6)	0

fication program. Only 4% require teaching methods courses which specifically indicate HIV/AIDS prevention education content for any program. (See Table 5.)

Requirements for Certification Programs

Most certification programs require few courses in the areas of health education, human sexuality education, or HIV/AIDS prevention education. Although elementary classroom teachers almost always have to deal with health education issues (Hausman and Ruzek, 1995), less than half of the schools (48%) require a health education course for preservice elementary teachers. Only 2% require a sexuality course, and only 3% require courses covering HIV/AIDS.

Figures indicate that preservice secondary teachers (those without a specific specialization in health or physical education) are far less likely to receive preservice training: only one in six schools (16%) require health education courses for preservice secondary educators, while only 1% require a sexuality course, and only 2% require a course covering HIV/AIDS. (See Table 6.)

Health and physical education teachers are most likely to provide sexuality education at the middle and high school level (Forest and Silverman, 1989). Preservice teachers enrolled in health or combined health and physical education certification programs are the most likely to be required to take courses in health education and sexuality. However, requirements differ among degree programs. Eighty-six percent of schools require a general health education course for preservice health educators[2] and 61% require a sexuality course. For preservice teachers in combined health and physical education programs, all schools offering such programs require health education, and 30% require sexuality education. Fifty-seven percent of schools require a health education course for preservice physical education teachers, while only 6% require a sexuality course.

Despite the great concern with HIV/AIDS in the 1990s, almost no schools require health or physical education preservice teachers to take a course covering this topic. No school requires preservice health education teachers to take a course covering HIV/AIDS. Only one school requires preservice physical education teachers to take a course covering HIV/AIDS, and one school requires preservice teachers enrolled in combined health and physical education programs to take such a course. (See Table 6.) In fact, only 12% of schools offer any courses covering HIV/AIDS. (See Table 3.)

Methods courses are even less likely to be required. Although one-third (35%) of schools require preservice elementary education students to take a health education methods course, none require a sexuality education methods course, and only 2% require a course that includes HIV/AIDS prevention education methods. Preservice secondary education students are even less likely to be required to take a health education methods course; only 4% of schools require it. No schools require sexuality education methods courses for preservice secondary educators, and only 1% of schools require courses that include HIV/AIDS prevention education methods. (See Table 7.)

TABLE 6. Percentage of Schools Requiring Subject by Certification Program

CERTIFICATION PROGRAM	PERCENT OF SCHOOLS REQUIRING HEALTH EDUCATION*	PERCENT OF SCHOOLS REQUIRING HUMAN SEXUALITY	PERCENT OF SCHOOLS REQUIRING HIV/AIDS EDUCATION
ELEMENTARY EDUCATION (N = 166)	48% (n = 80)	2% (n = 3)	3% (n = 5)
SECONDARY EDUCATION (N = 165)	16% (n = 27)	1% (n = 1)	2% (n = 3)
HEALTH EDUCATION (N = 69)	86% (n = 59)	61% (n = 42)	0
PHYSICAL EDUCATION (N = 108)	57% (n = 62)	6% (n = 6)	1% (n = 1)
HEALTH AND PHYSICAL EDUCATION COMBINED (N = 20)	85% (n = 17)	20% (n = 4)	5% (n = 1)
FAMILY LIFE EDUCATION (N = 3)	0	100% (n = 3)	0
OTHER TEACHER CERTIFICATION PROGRAMS (N = 10)	0	30% (n = 3)	0

*These figures exclude courses in first aid, nutrition, and other specific topics not relevant to human sexuality.

TABLE 7. Percentage of Schools Requiring Methods Courses by Certification Program

CERTIFICATION PROGRAM	REQUIRE HEALTH EDUCATION METHODS*	REQUIRE HUMAN SEXUALITY EDUCATION METHODS	REQUIRE HIV/AIDS EDUCATION METHODS
ELEMENTARY EDUCATION (N = 166)	35% (n = 58)	0	2% (n = 4)
SECONDARY EDUCATION (N = 165)	4% (n = 6)	0	1% (n = 2)
HEALTH EDUCATION (N = 69)	77% (n = 53)	9% (n = 6)	0
PHYSICAL EDUCATION (N = 108)	30% (n = 32)	3% (n = 3)	1% (n = 1)
HEALTH AND PHYSICAL EDUCATION COMBINED (N = 20)	100% (n = 20)	30% (n = 6)	5% (n = 1)
FAMILY LIFE EDUCATION (N = 3)	2 schools	3 schools	0
OTHER TEACHER CERTIFICATION PROGRAMS (N = 10)	10% (n = 1)	30% (n = 3)	0

*These figures exclude courses in first aid, nutrition, and other specific topics not relevant to human sexuality.

Even those teachers most likely to teach health, sexuality, and HIV/AIDS prevention education are not always required to take methodology and pedagogy courses in HIV/AIDS prevention and sexuality education. Although 77% of schools require preservice health educators to take a health education methods course, only 9% require a sexuality education methods course, and none require a course that includes HIV/AIDS prevention education methods. Preservice teachers in combined health and physical education programs are required to take health education methods courses in 85% of schools that offer such programs, but sexuality education methods courses are required in only 20% of schools, and courses including HIV/AIDS prevention education methods at only one school. Preservice physical education teachers are required to take health education methods courses in 30% of schools, but only 3% of schools require a sexuality education methods course, and only one school requires a course that includes HIV/AIDS prevention education methods. All three of the schools that offer a certification in family life education require a sexuality education methods course, but none require a health education methods course.

Key Concepts

A comprehensive sexuality education program covers human development, relationships, personal skills, sexual behavior, sexual health, as well as society and culture (National Guidelines Task Force, 1991). The majority of courses (90%) offered to preservice teachers list three or fewer of the key concepts. Human development, relationships, and society and culture are the most likely concepts included in course descriptions. Only 7% of schools list all six key concepts through some combination of courses offered; only four individual sexuality courses (1%) list all six key concepts in their course descriptions. In other words, preservice teachers in 93% of the institutions are unlikely to receive coverage of the six key concepts, even if they take every available course in a particular program.

Of the courses offered to preservice teachers:

- 4 cover all six key concepts;
- 33 cover four to five key concepts;

- 166 cover two to three key concepts;
- 143 cover one key concept;
- 39 were not specific enough to determine.

Of the courses required for at least one preservice certification program:

- no courses cover all six key concepts;
- 3 cover five key concepts;
- 1 covers four key concepts;
- 10 cover three key concepts;
- 15 cover two key concepts;
- 15 cover one key concept;
- 16 were not specific enough to determine.

Major Focus of Sexuality Courses

We also conducted a content analysis of course titles to supplement the course description analysis. While the course description may indicate a range of topics, the title itself indicates the central focus of the course. (See Table 8.) In some cases, the title also indicates the disciplinary or philosophical perspective from which the course is taught.

There were six general title categories for human sexuality courses: sex, sexual and sexuality; marriage, family, and relationships; gender/sex roles; reproduction/fertility; HIV/AIDS; and others (social problems/deviance, health, sexual assault or abuse, and gay and lesbian studies).

1. *Sex, sexual, and sexuality* (51%). There were 179 courses with the words "sex," "sexual," or "sexuality" in the titles, excluding those within the other specified categories. The majority were simply titled "human sexuality" or other variations. An additional 16 courses included "family life education" in the title, indicating a methods/teaching perspective. Only one course included "sexually transmitted diseases" in its title. Most course titles did not clearly identify a disciplinary or philosophical perspective. Of those that did, the greatest number were psychological (18 courses), followed by methodological (14 courses), religious/moral (10 courses), and sociological (8 courses).

TABLE 8. Focus of Human Sexuality Courses by Titles (N = 385)

FOCUS	PERCENT OF ALL HUMAN SEXUALITY COURSES
SEX, SEXUAL, AND SEXUALITY	51% (n = 195)
MARRIAGE, FAMILY, AND RELATIONSHIPS	34% (n = 131)
GENDER/SEX ROLES	7% (n = 26)
REPRODUCTION/FERTILITY	3% (n = 12)
HIV/AIDS	2% (n = 9)
OTHERS*	3% (n = 12)

*This category consists of courses falling into four categories: (1) social problems/deviance; (2) health; (3) sexual assault or abuse; and (4) gay and lesbian studies.

2. *Marriage, family and relationships* (34%). There were 131 titles (34%) that indicated a focus on relationships. The vast majority had the term "marriage and family" in their titles. Other relationship-related terminology included "courtship," "dating," "love," and "mate selection." Again, most of the titles did not indicate a disciplinary or philosophical perspective. Of those that did, a sociological perspective was most common (18 courses), followed by religious/moral (4 courses), psychological (2 courses), and methods/teaching (2 courses).

3. *Gender/sex roles* (7%). There were 26 courses (7%) with "sex roles" and/or "gender" in their titles. The most common perspective was psychological (5 courses), followed by philosophical (2 courses) and sociological (2 courses). One course each indicated a biological or religious perspective.

4. *Reproduction/fertility* (3%). There were 12 courses (3%) with a human reproduction or fertility focus evident in the titles. There were only two specific perspectives mentioned–biological (3 courses) and sociological (2 courses). Only one course title ("Natural Family Planning") specifically mentioned contraception.

5. *HIV/AIDS* (2%). There were nine courses (2%) with the words "HIV" and/or "AIDS" in the title. Of these, one course indicated a

psychosocial perspective; none indicated a methods/teaching perspective.

6. *Others* (3%). The remaining 12 courses (3%) fell into four categories: social problems/deviance, health, sexual assault or abuse, and gay and lesbian studies. Five titles mentioned social problems or deviance, with one from a religious perspective. There were four courses with health-related titles; only one indicated a methodological approach. Two titles mentioned sexual assault or abuse. One mentioned "lesbian/gay." This was the only course that indicated a focus on lesbian and gay issues or sexual orientation.

DISCUSSION AND RECOMMENDATIONS

The study's conclusions, while not surprising, show that there is still much work needed in the area of teacher preparation for HIV/AIDS prevention and sexuality education in the United States. While it is encouraging that almost all schools with teacher preparation programs offer at least one course in health education and sexuality issues, it is surprising and disappointing that few offer methodology courses and that only 12% have a course description that even mentions HIV/AIDS.

The findings clearly illustrate that preservice teachers are not adequately prepared to teach comprehensive HIV/AIDS prevention and sexuality education. Despite parental support and state-mandated demands for such education, those charged with this task do not have the proper tools to do so, leaving the responsibility to state and local departments of education and to the teachers themselves.

Specifically, only 14% of the surveyed institutions require health education courses for all of their preservice teachers and none require a sexuality course. For health education certification programs, only 61% of schools require sexuality courses and none require courses covering HIV/AIDS. For elementary, secondary, or physical education certification, almost no institutions require sexuality courses (2%, 1%, and 6%, respectively) or courses covering HIV/AIDS (3%, 2%, and 1%, respectively).

Preservice health educators are most likely to be required to take pedagogy and methodology training in sexuality education. Yet, only a minority (9%) of health education certification programs require a sexuality education methodology course. Previous research indicates that teachers with undergraduate preparation in areas other than health education are the most likely to teach these topics (Bensley and Pope, 1994; Forest and Silverman, 1989; Ballard, White, and Glascoff, 1990; Hausman and Ruzek, 1995; Levenson-Gingiss and Hamilton, 1989a). However, only 3% of physical education certification programs, and no elementary or secondary education certification programs required sexuality education methods courses.

The number of programs that require, or even offer, training in HIV/AIDS is even lower than for sexuality education. In their course descriptions for all preservice teachers, not a single school required a course that mentioned HIV/AIDS. Only 12% offer any courses that mentioned HIV/AIDS in their course descriptions. Even though most states have laws mandating HIV/AIDS prevention education in public schools, few colleges and universities provide their preservice teachers with the skills they need to provide such education.

Most preservice teachers have elective sexuality and health education courses available to them. However, highly structured programs often leave little time to take these courses. Even when students do have time, they will probably not find the courses comprehensive in scope; rather, the course will focus on one or two sexuality-related themes such as relationships, society and culture, or sexual development. Of the sexuality courses offered at the surveyed institutions, only four (1%) were comprehensive in scope, covering all six key concepts. We believe that teachers need such broadly focused courses in their preservice training to prepare them for teaching such courses to their own students.

Given the limitations of current offerings in preservice teacher education programs, we make the following recommendations:

- *Augment the number of sexuality and HIV/AIDS courses offered.* More colleges and universities should offer a complete course of study on human sexuality to preservice teachers. They should also offer courses covering HIV/AIDS. In addition, they should offer courses on the methodology and pedagogy of HIV/AIDS prevention and sexuality education.

- *Improve course requirements for health, sexuality, and HIV/ AIDS prevention education.* At the very least, those who will teach sexuality education should receive training in human sexuality (including HIV/AIDS prevention), as well as in the philosophy and methodology of sexuality education. Ideally, teachers should complete academic courses providing them with the most time-intensive and cognitively rich training. Professional preparation programs for all teachers should include at least one health education survey course, and one human sexuality course (including basic information about HIV/ AIDS). In particular, all elementary, health, and physical education teachers should be required to take courses on health education and sexuality education, as well as methods courses in these areas.
- *Expand the scope of courses.* Colleges and universities need to ensure that sexuality courses are comprehensive in scope. At a minimum, they should cover the six key concepts: human development, relationships, personal skills, sexual behavior, sexual health, and society and culture.
- *Enrich teacher certification requirements.* States should develop requirements that integrate sexuality education into existing health education certification requirements. Current requirements are not sufficient considering the vast number of professionals who are teaching sexuality education. Current credentialing and accreditation bodies should integrate HIV/ AIDS prevention education and sexuality education into their requirements for health educators.

CONCLUSION

Children and adolescents must have access to comprehensive health education, including HIV/AIDS prevention and comprehensive sexuality education. Future generations of teachers must acquire the knowledge and skills to empower children to make healthy decisions regarding sexuality, personal health, and interpersonal behavior. This study points to an immediate need in the United States to improve preservice teacher preparation in these critical areas.

NOTES

1. This organization's 700-plus member institutions comprise a broad cross-section of those preparing teachers across the United States and account for more than 85 percent of all new teachers entering the profession each year in the United States. Members range from very small religious colleges to large state universities located in all 50 states, the District of Columbia, the Virgin Islands, Puerto Rico, and Guam.

2. We would expect this figure to rise to 100% if health courses in nutrition, first aid, or other specific topics without sexuality information were included.

REFERENCES

Ballard, D., White, D., & Glascoff, M. (1990). AIDS/HIV Education for Pre-Service Elementary School Teachers. *Journal of School Health, 60*(6), 262-5.

Bensley, L.B., & Pope, A.J. (1994). A Study of Graduate Bulletins to Determine General Information and Graduate Requirements for Master's Degree Programs in Health Education. *Journal of Health Education, 25*(3), 165-171.

Carrera, M.A. (1972). Training the Sex Educator: Guidelines for Teacher Training Institutions. *American Journal of Public Health, 62*(2), 233-41.

Forest, J.D., & Silverman, J. (1989). What Public School Teachers Teach About Preventing Pregnancy, AIDS and Sexually Transmitted Diseases. *Family Planning Perspectives, 21*(2), 65-72.

Hausman, A., & Ruzek, S. (1995). Implementation of Comprehensive School Health Education in Elementary Schools: Focus on Teacher Concerns. *Journal of School Health, 65*(3), 81-85.

Kerr, D., Allensworth, D., & Gayle, J. (1989). The ASHA National HIV Education Needs Assessment of Health and Education Professionals. *Journal of School Health, 59*(7), 301-7.

Levenson-Gingiss, P., & Hamilton, R. (1989a). Evaluation of Training Effects on Teacher Attitudes and Concerns Prior to Implementing a Human Sexuality Education Program. *Journal of School Health, 59*(4), 156-160.

Levenson-Gingiss, P., & Hamilton, R. (1989b). Teacher Perspectives After Implementing a Human Sexuality Education Program. *Journal of School Health, 59*(10), 427-31.

National Guidelines Task Force. (1991). *Guidelines for Comprehensive Sexuality Education: Kindergarten–12th Grade*. New York: SIECUS.

Sexuality Information and Education Council of the United States. (1995). *SIECUS Review of State Education Agency HIV/AIDS Prevention and Sexuality Education Programs*. New York: SIECUS.

Sexuality Education in Seminaries and Theological Schools: Perceptions of Faculty Advocates Regarding Curriculum and Approaches

Sarah C. Conklin, PhD

SUMMARY. Sexuality education is included in professional career training but has not been comprehensively documented in seminaries and theological schools. This study's purpose was to explore and define sexuality education components in clergy training and to develop curricular implications based on faculty perceptions. The method was constructivistic inquiry authenticated by triangulation using three data sources: interviews, focus groups, and printed archives. Data included 39 semi-structured, narrative interviews with those providing exemplary education representing 9 faiths and denominations in 25 accredited U.S. institutions. Four focus groups

Sarah C. (Sally) Conklin is affiliated with the College of Health Sciences at the University of Wyoming.

Address correspondence to Sarah C. Conklin, School of Physical and Health Education, P.O. Box 3196, Laramie, WY 82071-3196.

The author is grateful for guidance from Dr. Charles Dwyer, Dr. Harold Lief, and Dr. Clyde Steckel.

The study was funded by the Center for Sexuality and Religion through support from Rev. Marta Weeks.

The study reported here is based upon a PhD dissertation at the University of Pennsylvania.

discussed condensed interview data, and archives were used to support and extend the results. Questions addressed extent, changes, limitations, and ideal visions of sexuality education for clergy students. A number of convergent themes emerged, along with some diversity of views and issues. Conclusions include recommendations for curriculum and professional education models, implementation strategies, and future study of sexuality issues in varied settings. *[Article copies available for a fee from The Haworth Document Delivery Service: 1-800-342-9678. E-mail address: getinfo@haworth.com]*

"Go talk to your minister." "Seek the advice of your clergyperson." "The priest may have a suggestion." "Ask the rabbi." "The chaplain can help." These statements sound typical of a newspaper advice column. They suggest seeking moral counsel and help in times of need from religious functionaries. For 153 million members of Christian denominations in the United States, belonging to nearly 340 thousand churches served by over 475 thousand clergy, religion is an integral part of life (Bedell, 1994, pp. 253-259). Their religious involvement may provide guidance in beliefs, practices, and moral codes of conduct. Issues concerning sexuality also permeate human lives and may result in both negative and positive outcomes. For many people, sexual beliefs and religious beliefs are intertwined. So, too, clergy and laity are linked throughout the life cycle as sexuality issues underlie many of the events, passages, and relationships that religion ritualizes, celebrates, and mourns. Trends over the past twenty-five years seem to indicate that clergy assistance regarding sexuality concerns is sought less than in the past, and that the help expected is less highly regarded (Gurin, Veroff, & Feld, 1960; Murstein & Fontaine, 1993; Rosser, 1991; Schindler, Berren, Hannah, Beigel, & Santiago, 1987; Veroff, Kulka, & Dorran, 1981).

The combination of interest and openness on the part of congregants and the availability of clinical training on the part of clergy has probably enabled some pastors to deal with issues of sexuality more comfortably and with greater knowledge. However, current attention to acting out and even abuse of various kinds suggests a need for seminaries to give more attention to the issues of sexual health. According to Richards (1992): "There is still no body of data or information that tells us how the seminaries themselves have adapted to the changes. . . . *A first step in this direction would be a well planned and carefully designed study of seminary curricula to determine how much or how little attention is being paid to sex education, sexual issues, and sexual health among students in the various seminaries and schools of theology throughout the United States"* [emphasis added] (p. 189).

Justification for sexuality education of clergy is based on the following three premises: that clergy will benefit from this education to fulfill their ministerial role as whole, healthy, fully-functioning persons; that their ability to be appropriately responsive to sexuality concerns within their communities and congregations will be enhanced by such education; and that clergy are sought out to provide religious perspectives on sexuality issues not available from secular helping professionals.

PURPOSE AND SIGNIFICANCE

This study explored the present status and definition of sexuality education within a particular setting–the seminary and theological school. Included were accredited U.S. institutions that provide post-baccalaureate education students preparing for careers as ordained or licensed religious functionaries, including priests, pastors, ministers, rabbis, chaplains, and pastoral counselors; they are broadly referred to as "clergy." In order to explore and define such sexuality education, expertise was sought from faculty members who have in the past or are now providing such clergy training. The overall perspective guiding this study assumed that:

- useful information leading to curriculum decisions is best gathered from those with experience and commitment to the topic under consideration,
- exemplary programs form the basis on which to build future recommendations,
- interaction among participants considering the content and methods of others is both generative and transformational, and
- curricular implications drawn from data gathered in collaborative ways will be more appropriate and acceptable than if collected otherwise.

METHOD

Design of the Study

Participants were selected by criterion-based researcher judgment. Through semi-structured narrative interviews with 39 informed observers, extensive and detailed information was gathered and coded. These data were thematically organized and anonymously presented to focus groups (attended by 3-6 interviewees in four locations) for reviewing, refining, and defining what has been, now is, and ideally should be sexuality education for clergy. Focus group results were analyzed for emerging concepts and relationships (Krueger, 1994; Morgan, 1993; Stewart & Shamdasani, 1990), resulting in curricular implications (both content and process). Also identified were resistances, limitations, and risks that might interfere with fulfillment of ideal sexuality education of clergy.

In qualitative inquiry, the researcher may be both participant and observer (Hammersley & Atkinson, 1983; Linn & Erickson, 1990; Reason & Rowan, 1981) as well as a learner (Glesne & Peshkin, 1992). Taking such a stance rather than acting as an authority can encourage respondents to be as forthcoming as possible.[1] As principal instrument of the study, the researcher brought a personal perspective and interpretive lenses through which all data were understood. The subjective nature of observing, recording, transcribing, and analyzing was recognized, even though the process of "bracketing" (Langenbach, Vaughn, & Aagaard, 1994, p. 364) was conscientiously attempted.

Time and Context

The research process was divided into four steps: (a) gathering data from individual interviews, (b) arranging and directing focus groups, (c) analyzing data (including archives), and (d) writing and reporting results. Of the 39 interviews conducted, 21 were face-to-face and 18 were by phone. The four half-day focus groups were held at seminaries willing to host the meeting, within convenient traveling distance for the participants, and during the daytime on a weekday to create a *natural* context. Locations spanned the United

States (east coast, west coast, midwest). Denominational and faith variation provided breadth (rather than randomness or typicality).

Participant Selection

As the primary source of data, the participants in the study were the key to its success. A group with the most expertise available on the topic of teaching sexuality in seminaries was sought. Criteria for participant selection included both faculty membership and sexuality teaching experience as well as variation (especially across faiths and denominations) and convenience (time availability and reasonable travel distance).

When participant identification actually began, suggestions from others expanded the pool to 101 potential interviewees. Selection criteria also were extended to include adjunct faculty status, being a graduate student in a teaching role, or being a denominational executive offering continuing education on sexuality issues. This more flexible application of the faculty status criterion was used for 15 of the 39 interviewees. The extended criteria provided a wider perspective in that all participants had expertise based on *teaching* (broadly defined) some aspect of human sexuality to clergy students. It included more than *courses* within traditional classroom settings (such as workshops, continuing education, lectures outside of classrooms, some small group seminars, and some one-on-one counseling or spiritual direction), and sexuality *content* was expanded to include teaching courses beyond those with sexuality in the title.

RESULTS

Characteristics of Participants

Some of the participants were reluctant to claim their sexuality teaching experience. Those in formal faculty positions identified themselves with various curriculum divisions within theological education, such as ethics, pastoral theology, or liturgics. Those who taught courses with sexuality in the title were immediately responsive, while those who incorporated sexuality issues or content within other courses expressed concern about whether they *belonged* in the study. For some, this reflected a definition of sexuality education as a named course or courses. For others, integration of sexuality content throughout the curriculum was a goal. The following examples of interviewee comments illustrate several views of what counts and what doesn't count as human sexuality education. The first capital letter is a code to identify the interviewee and the second letter identifies that person as female (F) or male (M).[2]

> EF: First of all, . . . let me repeat,. . . I do not look at myself as an educator. (p. 3, #12)

> FM: I remember the rector said to me,. . . "In your canon law *course,* [emphasis added] when you talk about subjects like impotency and things like that, could you give them a little course in anatomy?" I said, "Well, I know, that's the place for it" [integrated]. And he says, "I'm embarrassed," he says, "I recognize it" [the need for anatomy training]. (p. 23, #53)

> ZM: It's funny because when you called to ask about this and I said "Yes," I hung up the phone and said, "Why did I say 'yes' to that; I don't teach about sexuality!" (laughter) Then it was because I was thinking about courses. . . . She just got my name because I wrote that book [with sex in the title] and assumes that I teach [biblical] courses on this. And then as I got to thinking about it–it was a very interesting process, it was good to be pushed to think about it–I thought, "Oh, well actually I *do* [teach about sexuality]–Quite a lot!" Probably more than my colleagues, more than is happening at any other institution in [this group] I would guess. (p. 24, #71-73)

> GF: I mean, I don't *directly* teach human sexuality but I teach a course in Life Cycle, and in [that] course . . . when I teach weddings, I also teach gay and lesbian commitment ceremonies and other kinds of things. . . . (I don't even know this is quite about human sexuality but you said to say whatever was my first thought, so I'm going to . . .)–this may be totally useless for you. (p. 1, #4)

GF: Well, I don't, I don't *actually* teach human sexuality, so ... Would I want it to be a larger component of what we do? Perhaps ... It would be nice if students had more time to focus on issues of human sexuality. If it was very clear that the component of human sexuality was present in every course, and that teachers were all (in a more ideal future) all more conscious of it. That everyone paid attention to [it as] . . . an underlying issue. . . . I'd want awareness . . . in every course. (p. 11, #42)

DM: I teach a course in Foundations in Theological Ethics; I have a component on human sexuality in that course. The bulk of the course, we're really talking about . . ., but in the course I try to make it more practical, and talk about social problems. . . . [cites incest as an example], the problem of human sexuality and theology . . . (p. 2, #4)

These excerpts illustrate the range of seminary courses that incorporate sexuality content and also the reluctance of some participants to identify themselves as sexuality educators, perhaps because they perceive that label to fit only those who teach courses with *sexuality* in the title. Of the 39 interviewees in the participant group, 10 had the terms *pastoral, psychology, care,* or *counseling* in the title of their teaching area; 10 had the terms *spiritual,* or *theology* in their titles (4 had both); 8 had *ethics, moral* or *law* in the title; and 5 had *abuse prevention* as a focus. No particular discipline or title indicating teaching content seemed dominant among the participants, perhaps contributing to the feelings of isolation sometimes expressed in the interviews.

The descriptions in Tables 1, 2, and 3 quantify demographic information about the participants and the institutions they represented.[3]

Broad Themes

Four themes stood out most prominently from the interview and focus group data.

1. *Seek balance* between affirming sexuality's potential for health/vitality and caution against the possibility of harm/abuse.

2. *Emphasize integration* of (a) sexuality and spirituality with the goal of maturity in clergy role fulfillment, (b) sexual health and justice, particularly with respect to sexual orientation, (c) thinking and feeling in educating for wholeness, responding with compassion, and (d) multiple disciplines, recognizing the pertinence of sexuality for all theological study.

3. *Attend to unique contexts* by acknowledging variation and benefits of diversity in: (a) those who teach, (b) educational methods, and (c) resources used.

4. *Legitimate the content, need, and value of sexuality components* within seminary education by: (a) openly naming the content to overcome secrecy and denial, (b) encouraging institutional support through communication, and (c) commending/endorsing a community of scholars possessing specialized knowledge and skill relative to human sexuality.

The four themes reflect ideals regarding *content, goals, providers*, and *processes*, as well as *support* for clergy sexuality education. These themes can provide guidance for curricular decisions as seminary and theological school faculties seek to address aspects of human sexuality for clergy students.

Unity, Congruence, and Commonality Among Data

Each interview began in the following way: "I'd like to have you tell me (a story) about a time when you were teaching clergy students some aspect of human sexuality that you remember well because it stands out in your mind." This request elicited responses that were analyzed to address problem statements about *definition* such as: What is the status of sexuality education within professional training of clergy? How is sexuality education of clergy defined? What characterizes the sexuality education components that are offered? What outcomes are reported?

When the reported critical incidents were compared, similarities occurred in three primary areas: what the story was about, its affective character, and its context or setting. All participants responded with a narrative description (probably because a *story* was requested). Of those narratives, all but two placed the interviewee in a teaching, training, or observing role. In the two exceptions, *story*

TABLE 1. Participant Data

#	M/F	Age	Denomination	Ordained	Title
1	M	68	Baptist ABC	yes	Professor
2	M	59	Baptist BGC	yes	Professor
3	F	45	Disciples of Christ	yes	Executive Director
4	F	36	Episcopalian	yes	Priest/Student
5	M	47	Episcopalian	NA	Student/Instructor
6	M	48	Episcopalian	lay	Professor
7	M	52	Episcopalian	M.Div.	Assistant Professor
8	M	53	Episcopalian	yes	Professor
9	M	54	Episcopalian	yes	Priest
10	M	60	Episcopalian	yes	Professor
11	M	74	Episcopalian	yes	Retired Bishop
12	F	42	Jewish Reconstructionist	Rabbi	Director
13	F	36	Jewish Reformed	Rabbi	Instructional Coordinator
14	F	43	Lutheran ELCA	lay	Adjunct Faculty
15	F	47	Lutheran ELCA	yes	Assistant Professor
16	M	51	Lutheran ELCA	yes	Professor
17	M	65	Lutheran ELCA	yes	Retired Administrator
18	M	45	Presbyterian	yes	Clinical Director
19	F	56	Presbyterian	lay	Professor/Dean
20	F	62	Presbyterian	lay	Professor
21	M	74	Presbyterian	yes	Emeritus Professor
22	F	52	Roman Catholic	lay	Student
23	M	53	Roman Catholic	yes	Associate Professor
24	M	62	Roman Catholic	former OSB	Adjunct Professor
25	M	64	Roman Catholic	yes	Professor
26	F	65	Roman Catholic	Sister SSA	Faculty
27	F	79	Roman Catholic	Sister OSB	Lecturer
28	F	37	United Church of Christ	M.Div.	Director
29	F	47	United Church of Christ	yes	Adjunct Professor
30	M	49	United Church of Christ	yes	Associate Professor
31	M	53	United Church of Christ	yes	Professor
32	M	65	United Church of Christ	yes	Emeritus Professor
33	M	69	United Church of Christ	yes	Emeritus Professor
34	M	42	United Methodist Church	yes	Associate Professor
35	F	47	United Methodist Church	yes	Professor
36	F	49	United Methodist Church	lay	Professor
37	M	58	United Methodist Church	yes	Dean/Professor
38	M	72	United Methodist Church	yes	Emeritus Professor
39	M	NA	NA	NA	Assistant Professor
24	M	*		29 Ordained	24 Faculty
15	F	**		6 Lay ***	15 Other

* age range for males: 42-74 Average = 58, 1 did not report
** age range for females: 36-79 Average = 49.5
*** 2 did not report, 2 listed degree (M.Div.) but not ordination status

TABLE 2. Institution Data

#	Denominational Affiliation	Institution Location	Institution Size
1	Baptist ABC	east	large
2	Baptist ABC	west	small
3	Baptist BGC	midwest	large
4	Episcopalian	east	medium
5	Episcopalian	midwest	small
6	Episcopalian	west	small
7	Jewish Reconstructionist	east	small
8	Jewish Reformed	east	medium
9	Lutheran ELCA	midwest	very large
10	Non-denominational	east	large
11	Non-denominational	west	large
12	Presbyterian	midwest	large
13	Presbyterian	west	very large
14	Private	east	large
15	Private	south	large
16	Roman Catholic	east	small
17	Roman Catholic	east	medium
18	Roman Catholic	east	medium
19	Roman Catholic	midwest	medium
20	United Church of Christ	east	medium
21	United Church of Christ	midwest	medium
22	United Church of Christ	midwest	medium
23	United Methodist Church	midwest	large
24	United Methodist Church	west	large
25	United Methodist Church	west	large
east 10		small 5	
midwest 8		medium 8	
west 6		large 10	
south 1		very large 2	

Student enrollment by head count (HC) used to categorize institution size.

small	under 100 students
medium	100 to 300 students
large	300 to 600 students
very large	over 600 students

(Association of Theological Schools, 1995; Bedell, 1994; HEP, 1991)

TABLE 3. Academic Data

#	Teaching Area
1	AIDS, Anti-homophobia
2	Abuse Prevention
1	Biblio/poetry Therapy
1	Campus Ministry
1	Canon Law
4	Christian Ethics
1	Christian Social Ethics
1	Church and Society
1	Discovering Ministry
1	Interdenominational Administration
2	Liturgics
1	Moral Theology
1	New Testament
2	Pastoral Care
2	Pastoral Psychology
3	Pastoral Theology
1	Practical Rabbinics
1	Psychology
1	Religion and Society
1	Religion, Society, and the Arts
2	Sexual Abuse Prevention
1	Spiritual Direction
1	Spiritual Life/Psychology
1	Supervised Ministries
1	Theology and Ethics
1	Theological Ethics
1	Violence Prevention

seemed to be interpreted to mean *joke* or *anecdote* of a general nature.

Content of narratives. Many of the responses shared common content themes. The stories of critical incidents reported by most participants were alike in describing situations in which students expressed a high level of emotion regarding some sex-related experience in their lives. The interviewees also followed the description with an explanation of a general "rule," making the report a "signature story" (a distinctive set of characteristics making a condition or structure recognizable).

IF: When the . . . door closed, our little conservative [woman referred to earlier] started pounding the table and weeping and saying "That son of a bitch, that son of a bitch, I'd like to kill him." [She] proceeded to tell this horror story of [her] . . . lawyer husband [unintelligible] raping her. . . . That's an extreme case of what I have always found most interesting about teaching in a seminary . . . I always assume that extreme rigidity around issues of sexuality is tied to some unspoken crisis. . . . That's kind of typical . . . with teaching this–the immense gaps between people's public positions and their deepest feelings and experience . . . (p. 3, #4)

One aspect of content included in many stories was that of role–of the teacher, the student, and gender roles. Each of these descriptions added to the definition of sexuality education by indicating who did what, and how appropriately.

FF: Well, I rework the syllabus every year. Because I have new insights. They educate *me* as well as I instruct them. To be able to see the complexity of human awakening and struggle and so forth. It has given me a tremendous respect for these people who so trust that they are strong enough to look at this and to move with it. I love my work! It's not exclusively sexuality, you understand, it's really in spirituality. But it's a holistic spirituality. (p. 8, #16)

DM: I'm not a pastoral care person. I don't pretend to be. I'm a moral philosopher and I think the best part of wisdom is knowing your limits. I have no pretensions that I can be a surrogate therapist for anybody, you know, [for] any of my students who have suffered these sorts of things. [reference is to a student recognizing, naming, and seeking help regarding her own experience of incest] But I do see my role more as a kind of Socratic midwife.

SC: What a good metaphor.

DM: That helps perhaps to bring forth the thoughts . . . that are very difficult, that consist in thinking, discerning, deliberating about their experience in ways perhaps they never had before. I might be a first to help them give birth to new ideas and new personalities to process. That's how I pretty much see my role as teacher in the classroom. (p. 3, #14-16)

An advocate for using cases to expose students to a vast range of sexual behaviors explained his reasons:

> TM: . . . I'd learned before,. . . the importance of choosing one's case examples, (vignettes for study) . . . carefully to . . . expose them [students] to some of the things that really happen in the real world of human sexuality. In a way it's kind of shock therapy but it takes a lot of people . . . down off their illusions about ... how sexuality is or should be at least. The [case] study method is something I'm really committed to. (p. 16, #36)

Using cases for the purpose of more intense student involvement with the content was preferred over lectures by another interviewee:

> MF: I don't do real well with didactic lectures [especially] when I'm dealing with something as touchy as a pastor's . . . professional boundaries. I can lecture 'til I'm blue in the face, but they don't *own* that information unless they work a case study. So I use a lot of case studies, unless they somehow get it to surface in themselves. (p. 10, #35)

Other notable student situations reported in the critical incidents involved a physical handicap being transformed within the sexuality class (attributed by the professor to the freeing from anxiety that the class provided) (NM), a heterosexually married clergy person who revealed his homosexual orientation for the first time in a class (OM), an older woman student coming to terms with a widowed life devoid of intimate touching (QM), a group of college women confronting their male classmates about the inappropriateness of their concepts of rape and other forms of sexual violence (LM), and nine more incidents involving sexual orientation (BF, BM, CF, DF, GF, GM, HF, KM, XM).

Although the focus was on the students' high level of emotion, it was also clear that the interviewees themselves had strong feelings about the incidents they described. Often, the feelings seemed to be of concern about how well they had handled dramatic situations and the difficulty of teaching a "loaded topic" with "such deep personal ramifications" (LF, p. 3, #4).

> KF: So I'm not sure that I–as a teacher at those moments– processed that as effectively as I might have. (p. 3, #12)

> CM: I've had the awful opportunities of having to talk with *my* former students who have perpetrated [clergy sexual abuse] and have been [here] to talk about their issues. And, oh man,. . . it just makes me sick to my stomach to realize that I could have perhaps done more to help them–stay out of problems. . . . It's a heavy onus in one sense, and it's sort of frightening . . . but there's also motive to . . . keep this harmful stuff to a minimum,. . . as much as we can. (p. 8, #28-30)

> LF: Every once in a while [I] say, "Do you think we should teach that course again?" and we both go, "Oh, God, I can't handle it!" and I even told my women colleagues, "You guys, you're going to have to take your turn because [we] just don't feel capable of dealing with the level of stuff that gets washed up for people in this class." And SC, I have to tell you, I didn't feel we were presenting inflammatory material. We were doing this from an academic point of view and still . . . we decided not to teach it again on the basis of that. . . . I'd be interested to know whether [others] have the same sense of caution that I do. (pp. 3-4, #6)

Some commonalities regarding teacher role included the need for flexibility, acknowledgment of change according to time and circumstances, concern about the potential risks of teaching something so personal while also feeling a deep need to provide education which was eagerly sought and seen as helpful. All the interviewees expressed some degree of satisfaction and fulfillment in their work, as well as openness to continued learning. Resources (such as print, films, and guests) and at least one learning activity were mentioned by all the participants.

Another common theme concerned a search for balance or "some sort of middle ground" from which both detrimental and uplifting aspects of human sexuality can be examined. A prominent goal of providing opportunity while also maintaining safety echoed this theme of balance. Some contrasted the overly optimistic views that grounded their sexuality teaching in its early stages with their current caution–or even absence of current effort. Several expressed concern that the acknowledged negative effects of widespread sexual abuse and violence might cause them or others to lose sight of the need for knowledge and affirmation regarding sexuality.

Defining sexuality education by topic. Interview transcripts illuminated the nuances of roles, emotions, and expectations in classroom situations. However, a focus on *content*–noting descriptive words and their frequency–also revealed the subjects' views on sexuality education.

The most commonly mentioned concept involved sexual orientation. When the words *homosexual(ity)*, *heterosexual(ity)*, *gay*, and *lesbian* were tabulated, 31 of 36 transcripts contained at least one reference by the interviewee to one or more of these terms. One of the interviewees, who described himself as a gay man, mentioned one of the four sexual orientation terms 14 times in the interview. Another 21 interviewees used the terms from 3 to 8 times in their interviews. Other terms referring to sexual orientation were also counted. *Bisexual* was used by 7 interviewees, *transsexual* was used by 3, and *transgender(ed)* by 2. When word counts were combined with chosen topics, it became clear that sexual orientation was the most dominant aspect of human sexuality for the participants. Other concepts were also mentioned by many; however, none stood out as prominently as sexual orientation. The following excerpts clarify the context within which this issue arose.

> LF: As I perused the data quickly, I [noticed] an emphasis on sexuality as it is experienced by . . . persons in relationship. But I think there are some people for whom the study of sexuality is not going to have any merit until they see the structural implications in terms of social justice . . . in fact, for gay and lesbian people . . . seeking ordination,. . . they do not have an audience among many of the seminary administrators, [even those] (who have a liberal definition of themselves . . . who were very identified with the civil rights . . . or the

anti-war movements),. . . just don't see gay and lesbian identity as a justice issue. They see gay and lesbian identity as a search for personal fulfillment and so they do not approach gay and lesbian issues as political issues . . . (FGD, p. 23)

This interviewee pointed out a potential limitation to addressing issues of sexual orientation. If identity is viewed as an issue about personal fulfillment rather than social justice, its importance may be greatly diminished in the minds of some. Another interviewee identified the possibility of strong support for a "very left" (liberal or accepting) position toward variation in sexual orientation:

XM: You'll have people at seminary who are liberals by conviction, by personality-type or whatever, who become conservatives the minute this [issue of sexual orientation] surfaces, because they have to go fundraising. Now at 97, I don't know the trustees as well. . . . But [they] tend to assume that these issues cost money, in a sense, and that if you move in any of these directions, you are going to lose support. I beg to disagree. I think in this area [of the country] we could find [financial support] equally strong among radicals and liberals. And I think there are lots of people who would give money to a religious institution who is exceedingly left on these issues. (p. 8, #24)

Note that the term *sexual orientation* was not used in this excerpt, even though it was the topic being discussed. Perhaps concern about this issue (as it relates to religious institutions, clergy, and seminary education) was even more pervasive than word counts indicated; however, overt references may have been suppressed, due, in part, to recognition of church complicity in oppression regarding sexual orientation.

Other content themes included *gender, sexual violence* (grouped to include *rape, sexual abuse,* and *incest*), the closely related notions of *sexual misconduct* and *sexual harassment,* and *sexually transmitted diseases* (4), venereal disease (1), *HIV* (2), and *AIDS* (9). A cluster of terms unique to religious settings were mentioned by up to half of the participants, including *ordination, celibacy, sacrament, sexual ethics, sexual theology,* and *incarnation. Ordination* was mentioned by 11 interviewees. Of these, 2 clearly referred to ordination of gays and lesbians, 2 specified ordination of women as the concern, and 1 referred to both of these categories (orientation and gender). The term *celibacy* is faith specific. It was mentioned by 10 interviewees, all but one of whom were Roman Catholic (6) or Episcopalian (3). Historically, the issue of proscribed sexual activity for members of the Christian clergy has always been an aspect of identity. For purposes of clarity, celibacy is commonly defined as a "nonreproductive, nonsexually active stance in service of some group" (Sipe, 1995, p. 57). In this case, the group is the Roman Catholic Church. Celibacy was the predominant topic of the entire interview dialogue for 4 participants.

> GM: I don't think anybody can study the Catholic clergy without coming to the conclusion that the seminary system produces in relatively predictable proportions both those who will practice and those who will not practice celibacy. Those who come through the seminary system themselves violate the fiduciary responsibility in more or less predictable proportions, in more or less predictable ways as the system now exists. And I think that's a different way of looking at it,.... Now, does the system in any way contribute to the violation itself?
>
> SC: And what do you think?
>
> GM: I say, yes. I say that one of the questions is the characterological problem: How is it that someone who preaches ethics to others, and very, very firmly at times,. . . can split themselves off and live in this other way? That's . . . the problem of the doubling. . . . Within the Catholic church (and it may be in ministry generally) is the attraction *to* the ministry of a more rigid personality set: [one who] is going to be more prone to doubling than the more flexible personality set.

The previous interviewee was one of only a few who brought up the issue of institutional complicity in the problem of clergy misconduct. Otherwise, most of the participants viewed it strictly as an individual matter.

Significant events in the personal lives of students and clergy were identified as sexuality issues as well as religious issues. This supported the theme of integration, in which interconnections are made concrete through ritualized experiences which link classmates and families, clergy and congregants, individuals and God. In some ways, rites could be understood as a way in which religious ethics and personal ethics come together. Participants sought to emphasize sexual health, but it was elusive because of widespread recognition of the negative aspects of sexuality involving misuse of power. The positive aspects referred to included: understanding sexuality as a gift of God within an incarnational understanding of theology (divinity indwelling as flesh–the human body and all its senses being a created goodness), along with recognizing relational aspects of sexuality expressed in ways that involve mutuality, respect, and allowing choice and freedom from harm.

For some, the integration of sexuality and spirituality (connecting rather than separating body and soul as aspects of humanness) were interconnected with sexual wholeness and sexual health. Some relationship norms that could be applied to a definition of sexual health and wholeness included; "Is it loving? Is it fair? Is it self-liberating and is it self-giving? Does it enhance the joy of the other person? Does it allow for vulnerability?" (QM, pp. 12-13, #26). Another participant added trust, mutuality, equality of opportunity, and contribution to peoples' overall well-being (TM, p. 10, #24). He felt it important to have "a lot of grace involved . . . the kind . . . where people feel accepted even though . . ." (TM, p. 24, #52). If one overarching theme could be identified from all of the interviews, the most prominent was the search for balance in which the negative aspects of sexuality are acknowledged and addressed, but the positive potential of sexuality as a God-given gift for the purpose of human connection and joy is also affirmed.

Diversity and Uniqueness in Data

The previous section emphasized commonalities among the data; this section focuses on the contrasts, highlighting diverse and unique responses from participants. The interview and focus group transcripts were screened for variations that were evident in the use of language, composition, rhetorical style and mood. Particular emphasis was placed on metaphors that made each person's contributions unique. For example, a Baptist compared his job to keeping his thumb in a nearby dike, even though there are other leaks further away. He described dealing with so much clergy sexual abuse that "it's like drinking from a fire hydrant." A gentler and more optimistic view referred to doors and windows opening and students being led to a threshold but deciding for themselves whether or not to walk through. Another participant noted that "Sexual theology is the little key that picks the lock that opens the door on the big issues in seminaries."

The following excerpt is part of a unique story; this interviewee was the only one who referred to his advisory role in providing opinions to high church officials on matters of sexuality. Seeking this sort of informed opinion is unique to certain faiths and denominations (in this case, Roman Catholic):

> FM: This past week as a canon lawyer, a case was sent to me from the XXXXX office dealing with a transsexual, a *man,* at least anatomically a male, who had a sex change operation . . . and now wishes to marry in the XXXXX church. You know, I've been reading all week on this. It . . . saddened me very much because . . . we're dealing with perhaps people who are somewhat troubled. But I'm thinking to myself, this is a whole person, this is not just the person, you know, with a penis, or a person with a vagina, this is total soul ..., this is God's creation. Does God make a mistake? All these questions. And they're plaguing me, they're bothering me. . . . My conclusion when I sent it back to them, I said, "I think she ought to be allowed to marry." And as remarkable or as scandalous as it might be, I said I can't see any reasons for saying she *can't* marry. Because you know, it's a peculiar situation, there's no doubt about it, but I'm always reminded ... [of] Christ's words to the lawyers. Don't you lay such heavy burdens on the people's shoulders and do nothing to help to lift them. (p. 10, #21). . . . I think to myself, I'm a person who has twice gone through cardiac bypass surgery. And when people begin to argue about "It's against the law of nature," I say, "I am against the law of nature; [they] take my heart out and put me on a machine to keep me alive . . . so they can repair" [it]. I said, "I think that's

against the law of nature, too." So . . . I'm alive because of the miracles of that type of thing, that people have the genius to be able to make that type of *correction*. This [sex change operation] may be one of those situations [correction], and all the reading that I've done on it by professionals in the medical field–it all comes down to–they don't know. It's all *conjecture*. If you say, is this person that we're dealing with really a male or really a female,... they will say, "Well, on the one hand, and then on the other hand." And ..., the reason I reached the conclusion, I said, "We are swimming in a sea of doubt. And therefore, we ought to let her get married. Because we don't know." (p. 11, #25)

The careful ethical analysis required to this sort of decision could provide an interesting case study for students of any denomination. The arguments for and against using technology to correct a "mistake"–and whether or not that "mistake" is God's–raise complex theological questions, such as: "What is God's role in birth defects, illness, disease, and aging?" "What is our response in such situations?" "On what basis do we decide to take action?" For this participant, both reason (current medical opinion) and emotion (compassion) were considered, along with the words of Jesus recounted in the Bible and the value of tradition (natural law) as a guide. This excerpt is one example of the diversity, contrasts, and variations within the interview data.

Definitions and Visions

Definitions of sexuality education can be extrapolated from descriptions of critical incidents. The results might be summarized using a kaleidoscope analogy, as if the various aspects of the definition were pieces of glass inside a kaleidoscope, differing in size and shape. The largest pieces would be the ones brought up by the most participants, and the smallest pieces mentioned by the fewest. The kaleidoscope analogy could be extended by showing the variously shaped, sized, and textured pieces interacting together to form the basis of a mirrored design. In the hands of various faculty members at different institutions, the resulting pattern coming from the pieces interacting would be different. One could even imagine that the amount of light illuminating the patterns would differ and the rate of change caused by turning the kaleidoscope (considering or utilizing content) and allowing movement would vary at different institutions.

Respondents and discussants stressed the need to learn communication and interpersonal relationship skills to prepare for an adult ministry role as well as the need to exercise responsibility in defining and applying both sexual and professional ethics. Specifics of the proposed vision are included in the following excerpts in response to the interview question: What is *included in a vision* of sexuality education?

> HF: I think it would be wonderful if we reached a point where, in fact ... Sexual intimacy in a loving relationship was always acceptable, and . . . didn't have to be procreative in order to be meaningful. (p. 11, #33)

> YM: For me a theology of incarnation suggests that I have to see my sexuality as constitutive of who I am as a believer, not something I have to hide or escape from. And to the degree that we can communicate that to people, its liberating and it's also, I think, a significant step towards Christian maturity. Because I don't think one can be spiritually mature if one is schizoid. My sexuality is over here ... [hand gesture indicating separation]. (p. 16, #44)

> QM: What I ... would want in a course [is] to deal with definitional material. *What is sexuality?* And deal with social and psychological data we have about the character and shape of sexual expression among groups, among people. Deal with the psychological and the social understandings we have regarding special populations, whether we're talking about sexuality and the disabled or sexuality and the elderly. Indeed, all of us can be ... in one or more special populations. But the point is [that] I would like to see in a course great attention given to simply the descriptive, empirical explanation of what we do and don't understand about this phenomenon. And I say this because there are a lot of seminary students who want to jump over that. They want to jump *over* to the value side or to the analytical side. I think we ought to . . . talk about,. . . engage in the analysis, the critical assessment of . . . sex in America.

And be willing to look at both the way sexuality defines healthy existence, that is to say, the way it's there for people who go about normal, regular lives and ... is a part of those lives. In a relatively good fashion. But also ... break open and see . . . how sexuality does become negative and destructive. And I also think we ought to spend a lot of time on a constructive case . . . where we're trying to construct images of health, understandings of sexual expression and sexuality that hold out what we hope will be. And ought to be. And in turn should therefore affect social policy or churches' policies or the way we rear children; the way we relate to our spouses or our partners. And so those three–of description and analysis and critical assessment and constructive setting forth of important images of understandings–I think are the threefold aspects that ought to be there. (p. 12, #22)

What is *not included in a vision* of sexuality education? The following is illustrative:

HF: It would be wonderful if people weren't scared. I think people at this point are willing to be challenged only to a certain point and then they get frightened. Frightened that however they've defined themselves, or however they've been defined by others even as dependable or as clear as they believe it to be, and there would be a greater openness to the fact that the lines aren't all that clear. The fact that there is a great deal of gray area and that's a part of life. I wish people would recognize that there's a broad spectrum of sexualities and sexual expression, none of which is better than any other, but all of which make up a larger composite which is part of our humanity. (p. 12, #35)

Administrative concerns also could be graphically represented in the kaleidoscope pattern mentioned previously. Examples include: content being offered as a separate course or integrated into other courses or both; courses being elective, required for all, or denominationally required; starting points in various disciplines or fields, including ethics, human development, life cycle, pastoral care, or spirituality. The interaction of all aspects of the vision in the kaleidoscopic design would indicate that, under various circumstances, probably all the options could be accommodated; they need not be mutually exclusive.

CONCLUSIONS AND IMPLICATIONS

Based upon the material gleaned from the interviews and the focus group summaries, the following conclusions about sexuality education for clergy appear to be warranted. The conclusions are grouped according to questions addressed in the interview protocol.

Extent and Definition of Sexuality Education

Sexuality education for clergy is complex; it arouses strong feelings of concern on the part of students, faculty, administration, and members of various governing bodies. Further, it engenders intense efforts by faculty providers to write, prepare, present, understand, and respond in helpful ways to the benefit, learning, and growth of students toward personal wholeness and maturity in ministry roles.

Those who might be considered the "sexuality educators" in seminaries and theological schools are often reluctant to so name themselves; they use other disciplinary connections to identify their teaching roles. They lack scholarly organizations (except a few special interest groups within professional associations), journals, and academic recognition in the area of sexuality. They express anxiety about how their teaching of sexuality content will be viewed by others.

In spite of apparent lack of support, sexuality courses and content are sought by students, even though not required. They seem to be positively evaluated and to fill an important formational role in the students' development toward awareness, insight, and maturity. However, the value of sexuality content as necessary and useful preparation for clergy roles may not be recognized by students until after graduation, when their careers have begun.

Sexuality content frequently engenders a high degree of emotional involvement, passion, and concern. Currently, potential for harm seems to be the criterion on which greatest priority is placed. Balance is sought; however, resources, language, and experiences (both personal and educational) that focus on positive aspects of sexuality seem to be lacking.

Changes in Sexuality Education

Profound changes in sexuality education have occurred in the past three to four decades. Original resources are outdated; more commercial films, popular literature, and case studies are now used. Printed materials with sexuality content, both scholarly and popular, have vastly increased in number and quality. The Sexual Attitude Reassessment (SAR) model–combining intense exposure to sexually explicit media and representatives of varied sexual lifestyles with small group discussion–is still controversial, regarded with enthusiasm by some and with suspicion by others. For a variety of reasons, sexuality education using this model is less available to clergy now than in the two previous decades. Increased awareness of the pervasiveness of negative aspects of sexuality has provided the impetus for continuing education requirements, mandatory screening evaluations, and development of training programs focusing on prevention of various kinds of sexual boundary violations.

The student body in seminaries has become older and more diverse in gender and ethnicity, with more part-time and second-career students. Students also appear to be more varied in attitudes, more willing to share personal experiences, and more open about sexual orientation (though some participants did not share these perceptions).

Visions for Sexuality Education

The ideal situation described by participants is based upon a changed understanding of human nature–particularly relations between males and females. A profound reformation in behavior and values underlies a cultural revolution in which movement toward a just and caring world could include a nonrepressive approach to sexuality. More honest and direct engagement of sexuality issues by the entire theological community is needed as part of the fundamental paradigm shift now occurring, in which the interrelation of all humans without oppression is viewed as a mandate.

Strategies and processes envisioned include the following suggestions: More than one course is desirable, perhaps offered as continuing education and/or by several cooperating institutions. Courses should lead people into safe spaces where they can take risks, participate in dialogue, and deliberate significant moral questions related to human sexuality. Goals include working out theological responses to a variety of challenging sexuality issues. Retreats or intense experiences such as SARs can allow personal issues to surface and be dealt with early in students' training, followed by opportunities–through case studies, for example–to focus cognitively, professionally, and strategically on sexual issues that will be encountered in future career settings.

Those who provide clergy education and training need to be comfortable with their own sexuality, respectful of the sexuality of others, as well as open, tolerant, and able to discuss without judgment–and have an appropriate sense of humor. Further, sexuality educators of clergy should have a solid theoretical grounding in sexual science, know its language and literature, be sensitive to diversity issues, and be able to work with an interdisciplinary team of mixed genders and sexual orientations.

Ideally, the enriched resources available to support sexuality education should be multidisciplinary, up-to-date, scientifically sound, and reflect diversity (experientially, sociologically, theologically, and ethnically). Further, a commitment of sufficient *time* for reflection and processing by students is critical.

The content of sexuality education should be structured around pastoral issues and grounded in ministry experience. It should provide attention to sexuality generally, sexual violence and abuse specifically (as well as more subtle boundary violations), and information about a range of sexual variations. Sexuality education should be integrated with spiritual guidance. Hopefully, students can be attracted to sexuality courses whatever their theological orientation (liberal or conservative), and they should be able to come away from such education comfortable, erudite, knowledgeable, effective in biblical work, and prepared for the challenges of sexuality concerns and issues that they will face in congregations.

Resistance to Sexuality Education

When denominational committees have tried to articulate theological positions on various sexuality issues, they often have come to great grief over their efforts. The ensuing divisive controversy is feared because of perceived detrimental effects–particularly financial–keeping both individuals and institutions defensively immobilized.

Like other sexuality educators, many seminary faculty seek value satisfaction, such as peer acceptance, job security, and peace of mind regarding the well-being of their students. To the extent that they perceive sexuality education interfering with these needs, such education will be restricted or resisted. For their part, students may resist dealing with sexuality content in classes for various personal reasons, such as beliefs, values, or fears (of disclosure, the unknown, or offending others), as well as in response to societal or denominational pressures and time limitations.

Broad-based support for sexuality education seems lacking, except as professional liability insurers encourage risk reduction measures to prevent actionable behaviors which could lead to malpractice claims. Nevertheless, some recognition of need is expressed, and some faculty efforts are supported. Some administrators are positive (particularly in response to student or peer pressure); however, this support is far outweighed by administrative indifference or caution (though outright hostility is perceived as decreasing).

Support for Sexuality Education

Faculty members expressed optimism about their own efforts and general support for their peers teaching sexuality content. At the same time, there remain fundamental questions about the mysteries of sexuality itself, as well as about the ability of churches to respond appropriately to human needs in this area, and of U.S. society's capacity to develop images, models, networks, and ways of living that allow the pluralistic experiment which is American democracy to thrive. These educators express concern about whether it is possible to hold personal experience in creative tension with religious vision, and whether the importance of sexuality can be affirmed without giving it undue or distorted emphasis.

The pioneering work of educating and writing about sexuality in religious contexts during past decades is revered by those who have participated and by their colleagues. A high standard has been set, and the impetus to do more, not less, is apparent. However, what there should be *more of* is not clearly articulated as a unified plan of action; planning and development are open-ended. There is eagerness and enthusiasm–extending far beyond polite interest from students, congregants, and clergy–to have sexuality issues addressed openly and to move in the direction of health, justice, and wholeness.

Participants in this study expressed their sense of being somewhat isolated and often without support in their efforts. They described strong commitments to teaching about sexuality and beliefs in its necessity for students. Indeed, participants were mostly eager to cooperate in the study, to share their expertise, to interact with their peers in focus groups, and to request results. This willingness may reflect the need to be affirmed in work that is perceived as risky and unrecognized. Such recognition, along with peer interaction opportunities, could be facilitated in practice by computer networking, regional meetings, denominationally supported exchanges, and task-focused collaborative efforts across institutional and disciplinary lines.

Practical Implications

Gatherings of faculty members could provide institutional recognition, legitimization of content, publication opportunities, valuable affirmation, and sharing of experiences. Mandating sexuality education with a uniform curriculum was deemed unrealistic–and unlikely to be implemented. Yet, several suggested that a course be required or that content about sexuality should be included by everyone on a faculty in whatever courses they teach. Efforts to create a uniformly acceptable model appear misguided due to institutional diversity. Increasing the sexuality components available to clergy students might be a better strategy.

Perceived adverse pressure or lack of support for sexuality education from external sources (such as denominational representatives, school administrators, trustees, or congregants) is a concern. Fear of controversy and attendant negative outcomes seemed to motivate much of the concern about external resistance. A slight change in attitude might lessen the immobilizing influence of such perceptions. Controversy could be viewed as having some potential benefits, such as giving voice to varied opinions and diverse attitudes, providing an opportunity for shared learning and growth, moving toward a more just, equitable and respectful position, providing needed and desired openness and communication. Another shift in viewpoint would be to recognize that controversy about sexuality is inevitable, regardless of what educational effort is proposed or pursued. Indeed, raising controversial issues need not be seen as detrimental; when supporters are reluctant to speak out, controversy is sometimes the very thing needed to bring them forward.

Future research on clergy sexuality education could include more diversity in faiths and denominations of those surveyed or interviewed. In addition, designing a relatively simple instrument to assess seminary students' perceived needs and interests might open the door to justifying content that would otherwise be rejected. It seems that responsiveness to student concerns is one of the strongest motivations of faculty members and administrators of most faiths and denominations.

If money, time, and expertise are to be directed toward pilot program development or creation of a model for sexuality education, then groups of interested participants must work cooperatively to develop consensus on high priority needs. One such need mentioned often by participants in this research is how to involve reluctant students in sexuality education. The career-based expertise of those who have maintained high enrollments in sexuality classes over many years would be helpful input for devising strategies to attract such students and encourage their participation. Another concern expressed was the need for up-to-date, culturally sensitive audiovisual materials. Many printed resources were recommended by interviewees. Publications do not seem to be lacking–except that most emphasize sexual harm rather than sexual health.

Several participants discussed the merits of having students develop liturgical rites relative to sexuality issues. Providing forums for students with similar concerns across denominations and faiths might be a productive ecumenical strategy. Those who are currently providing sexuality education, or have done so in the past, could be organized to recruit others for such teaching. One of the benefits of diversity among faculty members doing sexuality education is the broad network of contacts their affiliations create.

Theoretical Implications

The first implication derives from the need for a *balance* in emphasis between sexual health and sexual harm. In an effort to prepare mature and effective clergy, this balance requires a "two-pronged" approach: Prevention strategies need further study and implementation, while emphasis on criteria for sexual health and justice also must be pursued vigorously–particularly as potentially articulated in a sexual theology.

A second theoretical implication arises from the emphasis on relationships that was clearly conveyed by most of the interviewees. A key point is the transition from form-centered norms (such as age, gender, or marital status) toward norms based on relational criteria for judging sexual behavior. This change was described by James B. Nelson (1988) as "a shift from an act-centered sexual ethics to a relational sexual ethics" (p. 124). "Mutuality," "respect," and "well-being" were terms used repeatedly by participants, particularly in their statements of vision, often in describing their commitment to rites for same-sex unions. Further articulation of this perspective is needed if it is to become an effective means for promoting sexual justice and emphasizing relational ethics for both clergy and congregants.

A third implication relates to the importance of multidisciplinary interaction and cooperation in the development and implementation of sexuality education within seminaries and theological schools. The participants in this study clearly affirmed diversity and pluralism as positive attributes in clergy education, and they often described the benefits of team teaching. Cooperative teaching across disciplinary lines may be one answer to Kelsey's (1993) concern that theological education needs "some alternative conceptuality, hopefully one that is modest and unelaborate, [to] clarify where conventional terms obscure, [which will] allow us to pose fresh and productive questions where conventional questions have proven unfruitful" (p. 229).

CONCLUSION

There is a continuing need to legitimize sexuality education as a necessary and efficacious part of seminary and theological school training for both personal enhancement and expedient performance of the clergy role. The goal of ongoing interaction among involved experts may lead to openly naming and articulating the pervasiveness of sexuality concerns for all theological study, as well as developing a conceptual scheme for theological education in which sexuality is a hub and institutional support is solid. As the data demonstrate, this has both theoretical and practical implications. The results of this inquiry suggest the importance of *balance* between positive and problematic aspects of sexuality, along with an emphasis on *integration* of disciplines, concepts, and methods. At the same time, future efforts should reflect *diversity* and *flexibility*; varying approaches, methods, and resources are needed for sexuality education of clergy of differing faiths, beliefs, ethnicities, ages, personal backgrounds, and life situations.

NOTES

1. A research partner with expertise in communication and theology was incorporated in the design as co-inquirer to extend the data analysis done by the primary researcher whose training emphasized education and psychology. This analytic extension followed the suggestion of Janesick regarding researcher role in qualitative inquiry. It needs to be described thoroughly and recognized as a critical perspective in the report writing. She recommended several kinds of triangulation: the addition of the research partner incorporated both *investigator* triangulation as "the use of . . . different researchers or evaluators" and *interdisciplinary* triangulation "which will help to lift us out of the . . . trench [in which] psychology has dominated educational discourse altogether" (Janesick, 1994, pp. 214-215). Aspects of narrative inquiry were included in the research design through literary and rhetorical analysis to establish fidelity as a criterion in the use of stories (Blumenfeld-Jones, 1995; Connelly & Clandinin, 1990).

2. When interview and focus group transcripts are quoted directly, the coding protects anonymity while providing an audit trail to a particular citation. The interviewee's name is represented by a bold upper case initial (arbitrarily assigned) followed by "M" for male or "F" for female. Initials "SC" represent the interviewer (primary researcher). The parenthetic reference following each citation indicates the source page and paragraph number(s) in the participant's transcript. Quotes from focus group transcripts have a group code (FG A-D) with the page number.

Names of states, cities, institutions, denominations, and others are coded using lower case letters and numbers. Some generic terms and denominations are represented by Xs. Some numbers and dates are eliminated to protect confidentiality and are represented by ___. Two kinds of ellipses may occur in quotations. If the transcriber left out some word(s) (as unintelligible or extraneous), there are no spaces between the periods (...). If transcribed words or sentences are omitted by the writer/researcher (for clarity or brevity), there are spaces between the periods (. . . for omitted words and . . . . for omitted sentences). Inserted words or explanations added within quotations are bracketed conventionally.

3. In tables, the individual participant names are replaced by numbers from 1 to 39 (Table 1) and institution names are replaced by numbers from 1 to 25 (Table 2). There are fewer institutions than participants because some participants were affiliated with denominations or organizations other than schools. Some institutions had more than one faculty member participating. When categorizing institutional size for the purpose of this study, size conventions used by members of the ATS were followed. Locations of institutions were reported by grouping states into regions; CT, MA, MD, NJ, NY, and PA are east; IL, MN, and OH are midwest; FL and TN are south; CA and CO are west.

REFERENCES

Association of Theological Schools (1995). *Directory from Bulletin 41, Part 4.* Pittsburgh, PA: ATS.

Bedell, K. B. (Ed.). (1994). *Yearbook of American & Canadian churches 1994.* Nashville, TN: Abingdon Press.

Blumenfeld-Jones, D. (1995). Fidelity as a criterion for practicing and evaluating narrative inquiry. *International Journal of Qualitative Studies in Education,* 8(1), 25-35.

Connelly, F. M., & Clandinin, D. J. (1990). Stories of experience and narrative inquiry. *Educational Researcher, 19*(4), 2-14.

Glesne, C., & Peshkin, A. (1992). *Becoming qualitative researchers: An introduction.* White Plains, NY: Longman.

Gurin, G., Veroff, J., & Feld, S. (1960). *Americans view their mental health.* New York: Basic Books.

Hammersley, M., & Atkinson, P. (1983). *Ethnography principles in practice.* London: Routledge.

Janesick, V. J. (1994). The dance of qualitative research design: Metaphor, methodolatry, and meaning. In N. K. Denzin & Y. S. Lincoln (Eds.), *Handbook of qualitative research.* Thousand Oaks, CA: Sage.

Kelsey, D. H. (1993). *Between Athens and Berlin: The theological education debate.* Grand Rapids, MI: Eerdmans.

Krueger, R. A. (1994). *Focus groups: A practical guide for applied research.* Thousand Oaks, CA: Sage.

Langenbach, M., Vaughn, C., & Aagaard, L. (1994). *An introduction to educational research.* Boston: Allyn and Bacon.

Linn, R. L., & Erickson, F. (1990). *Research in teaching and learning, Volume 2: Quantitative methods, Qualitative methods.* New York: Macmillan.

Morgan, D. L. (Ed.). (1993). *Successful focus groups: Advancing the state of the art.* Newbury Park, CA: Sage.

Murstein, B. I., & Fontaine, P. A. (1993). The public's knowledge about psychologists and other mental health professionals. *American Psychologist, 48*(7), 839-845.

Nelson, J. B. (1988). *The intimate connection: Male sexuality, masculine spirituality.* Philadelphia: Westminster.

Reason, P., & Rowan, J. (Eds.). (1981). *Human inquiry: A sourcebook of new paradigm research.* Chichester: John Wiley & Sons.

Richards, D. E. (1992). Issues of religion, sexual adjustment, and the role of the pastoral counselor. In R. M. Green (Ed.), *Religion and sexual health: Ethical, theological, and critical perspectives.* Norwell, MA: Kluwer.

Rosser, B. S. R. (1991). *Male homosexual behavior.* New York: Praeger.

Schindler, F., Berren, M. R., Hannah, M. T., Beigel, A., & Santiago, J. M. (1987). How the public perceives psychiatrists, psychologists, nonpsychiatric physicians, and members of the clergy. *Professional Psychology: Research and Practice, 18,* 371-376.

Sipe, A. W. R. (1995). *Sex, priests, and power: Anatomy of a crisis.* New York: Brunner/Mazel.

Stewart, D. W., & Shamdasani, P. N. (1990). *Focus groups: Theory and practice.* Newbury Park, CA: Sage.

Veroff, J., Kulka, R. A., & Dorran, E. (1981). *Mental health in America.* New York: Basic Books.

Trends in Sexuality Education in United States and Canadian Medical Schools

Marian E. Dunn, PhD
Pierre Alarie, MD

SUMMARY. There has been a concern that earlier gains in the teaching of human sexuality in medical schools may have eroded in recent years. An extensive survey of 109 U.S. and 13 Canadian medical schools revealed that a dramatic decrease in the number of curriculum hours devoted to human sexuality has not occurred. In fact, 28% of U.S. and 36% of Canadian schools have actually increased hours, and ninety-two percent of all medical schools responding currently offer core curriculum material in sexuality, averaging approximately 11 hours in U.S. and 18 hours in Canadian schools. Unfortunately, nearly a third of schools in both countries do not specifically address important health issues, such as sex and illness or disability, and some schools even neglect training in the taking of a sexual history. Data on these issues is important for making future decisions regarding the contents of the increasingly overburdened medical curriculum. *[Article copies available for a fee from The Haworth Document Delivery Service: 1-800-342-9678. E-mail address: getinfo@haworth.com]*

Marian E. Dunn is affiliated with the Center for Human Sexuality, Department of Psychiatry, State University of New York at Brooklyn. Pierre Alarie is affiliated with the Sexual Dysfunction Center, St. Luke's Hospital, Montreal, Canada.

Address correspondence to Dr. Marian E. Dunn, Box 1203, Department of Psychiatry, SUNY, 450 Clarkson Avenue, Brooklyn, NY 11203.

[Haworth co-indexing entry note]: "Trends in Sexuality Education in United States and Canadian Medical Schools." Dunn, Marian E., and Pierre Alarie. Co-published simultaneously in *Journal of Psychology & Human Sexuality* (The Haworth Press, Inc.) Vol. 9, No. 3/4, 1997, pp. 175-184; and: *Sexuality Education in Postsecondary and Professional Training Settings* (ed: James W. Maddock) The Haworth Press, Inc., 1997, pp. 175-184. Single or multiple copies of this article are available for a fee from The Haworth Document Delivery Service [1-800-342-9678, 9:00 a.m. - 5:00 p.m. (EST). E-mail address: getinfo@haworth.com].

The physician is often regarded by lay people as the professional most competent and knowledgeable about sexual concerns. In the 1970s, attention was focused on the sexuality education offered to medical students in the hope that effective training would improve the preparation of physicians for this role (Lief, 1971). Over the next decade several studies were undertaken to review course offerings and outcomes (Garrard, Vaitkus, Held, & Chilgren, 1976; Lamberti & Chapel, 1977; Lloyd & Steinberger, 1977; Marcotte, Geyer, Kilpatrick, & Smith, 1976). With the advent of H.I.V. as well as the dramatic increase in S.T.D. and reports of sexual abuse, preparation of future physicians seems even more important. Moreover, with increases in life expectancy, recognition of the sexual side effects of a host of modern treatments and medications, and the greater role of the primary care physician in the delivery of health care, the need for effective sexuality training during the medical school years has assumed increasing significance. Nevertheless, there is concern among sex educators that in this more conservative era, sexuality education in medical schools has been dramatically decreased or eliminated. This study was undertaken to assess this issue.

METHODOLOGY

Under the auspices of the Consortium of Sex Educators in the Health Professions, a twelve-item questionnaire was mailed to 130 U.S. medical schools and to the 16 Canadian medical schools. The survey was directed to the deans of medical education, and curriculum. Topics included: school name; contact person; whether the school offers required sexuality courses, subsections of courses, or isolated lectures on sexuality; department(s) responsible for the teaching; in which course(s) material was offered; number of hours of instruction; the year(s) in which instruction was offered; whether offered in clerkship(s); number of hours; in which year(s); topics covered; teaching format; elective offerings; and were hours expanded, decreased or maintained for past few years; additional comments. After four months a second request was mailed to schools that had not responded. A third request via telephone and fax was made two months later. Survey questions were developed by the senior author and pretested on colleagues for clarity. A copy of the full questionnaire is available upon request from the senior author.

RESULTS

Of the 130 U.S. schools contacted, replies were received from 111 schools (85%). Nineteen schools failed to respond; two schools submitted the survey with most items missing so that their responses were eliminated. In addition, four schools noted that their curricula were in transition to problem-based learning (a new teaching modality that eliminates all formal courses). Thus, reasonably complete data was provided by 105 U.S. medical schools, although not every item was completed for each institution. Of these, 100 (95%) indicated that they offered core curriculum, non-elective classes in sexuality. Five schools had no such classes.

Responses were also received from 14 (88%) of the 16 Canadian medical schools. Again, not all responses were complete. Of these, 13 (93%) offered core curriculum classes in sexuality. The other Canadian medical school utilized a Problem-Based Learning approach and offered no specific classes to students.

Class Hours Devoted to Sexuality

As seen in Table 1, the U.S. schools had a mean of approximately 11 hours spent on sexuality material, whereas in Canada the mean number of class hours was 18.5. The majority of U.S. (59%) and

TABLE 1. Sexuality Teaching–Class Hours

U.S. (N = 100)	Canada (N = 12)
X = 11.3 hours	X = 18.5 hours
Bimodal = 4, 16	Bimodal = 16, 18
median = 10	median = 16
range = 0-40	range = 6-45

Canadian schools (55%) reported no changes in class hours offered in recent years. Class hours have been expanded in recent years in 26 (28%) of the American schools and in 4 (36%) of the Canadian schools. Class hours were decreased in 12 (13%) of U.S. schools and in 1 (9%) Canadian school. Of twelve U.S. schools reducing hours, eight still retained between 8 and 24 hours (an average of 11 hours) while the one Canadian school that decreased hours maintained 22 hours devoted to sexuality in its curriculum.

Elective class hours were offered by 30 (30%) of the U.S. and 6 (46%) of Canadian schools. In all of the schools that offered electives, these courses were *in addition* to the core curriculum courses.

Timing of Sexuality Classes

While there is variation in the year in which sexuality courses are offered to medical students, the majority of U.S. schools (79%) focus their teaching in the first or second year. Only 21% of schools offer material after these preclinical years (Table 2). This appears less common in Canada, where only 38% of schools offer classes during years one and two. In Canada, 62% of schools include sexuality classes after the second year of study.

Responsibility for Teaching

Sexuality education is provided on a multidisciplinary basis (i.e., with several departments sharing responsibility) in 39% of U.S. and

TABLE 2. Class Years in Which Sexuality Is Taught

	U.S. (N = 100)	Canada (N = 13)
Only in 1st	22 (22%)	0
Only in 2nd	20 (20%)	4 (31%)
In 1st & 2nd	37 (37%)	1 (5%)
Total Preclinical Years	79 (79%)	5 (38.4%)
After 2nd Year	21 (21%)	8 (61.5%)

31% of Canadian schools. Departments of Psychiatry have primary responsibility for sexuality teaching in another 38% of U.S. schools, but only in 23% of Canadian schools. In Canada, Family Medicine has the main teaching responsibility in 31% of schools while in the U.S., Family Medicine provides the teaching in only 7% of schools. Obstetrics/Gynecology is responsible in 6% of U.S. schools and in 15% of Canadian schools. Various other departments, such as Geriatrics, Medicine, Urology, Neurology, Internal Medicine, Basic Science, Medical Ethics, and the Dean's office, had major responsibility for this teaching in a subgroup of schools.

Coverage of Topics

As shown in Table 3, the subject matter of these courses is quite broad in most schools. Seventy-three percent of U.S. and 62% of Canadian schools cover eight or more topics concerned with sexuality. At least six different topic areas are covered by an additional 10% of U.S. and 23% of Canadian schools and four to five topics are covered by another 10% and 15%, respectively. In the U.S., only

TABLE 3. Topics Covered in Sexuality Teaching

1) Sexual anatomy and physiology

2) Sexual dysfunctions

3) HIV/AIDS

4) Homosexuality/bisexuality

5) Paraphilias

6) Taking specific sex history

7) Sex/illness/surgery

8) Sex/disability

9) Cultural differences in sexual behavior

10) Relationship and intimacy issues

11) Gender dysphorias

7% of schools offer sexuality instruction covering three or fewer topics. While this education is being provided to prospective physicians, some areas are ignored. Thirty-one percent of U.S. and 31% of Canadian schools do not specifically address issues of sex and illness and/or disability, and 8% of U.S. and 15% of Canadian schools do not specifically teach students to take a sexual history. While most schools teach about H.I.V., the broader topics of homosexuality and bisexuality are not dealt with by 6% of U.S. and 15% of Canadian schools.

Teaching Methods

The majority of U.S. (78%) and Canadian (82%) schools use a combination of teaching modalities for this material which include, in addition to lectures, small groups, panels, patient interviews, invited guests (for example, homosexual or transgender individuals), films/videos, and workshops. Small group discussion is a particularly popular teaching strategy, with this technique chosen by 87% of U.S. and 100% of Canadian schools. Sexually explicit films and videos are used in 47% of U.S. schools and in 50% of Canadian schools. Less explicit, informational films/videos are utilized in 73% of U.S. and 75% of Canadian medical schools.

DISCUSSION

Contrary to our initial expectations, medical schools in both Canada and the U.S. *did* seem committed to providing sexuality education to medical students. We did not find a dramatic decrease in programs. In 1975, Lief and Ebert reported that 60% of U.S. schools had core curriculum courses in sexuality, while in 1984, Cross et al. reported that 82% of schools offered core curriculum classes. Today, 95% of the U.S. schools and 93% of the Canadian schools responding to our survey offer core curriculum courses in sexuality. By contrast, only 70% of schools in the United Kingdom offer such programs (Reader, 1994).

Direct comparison of class hours over time is more difficult; in each of the previous studies, class hours were assessed differently.

In 1975, Lief and Ebert indicated more class hours than are currently offered; however, their data included elective as well as required hours. In 1980, Lloyd and Steinberger found that schools with specific sexuality courses averaged a greater number of class hours (23 hours) than programs where there was a fragmented presentation of material (18 hours). In that study, however, Lloyd and Steinberger included class hours spent on reproductive biology as well as on specific sexuality topics. By 1984, Cross and colleagues found medical schools devoting an average of only 12 hours to sexuality material. This is consistent with our U.S. findings in 1995. We are not aware of any previous Canadian studies, so we are unable to examine trends in Canadian schools.

When we compare programs in the U.S. and Canada, some interesting differences emerge. The Canadian schools not only currently offer more class hours than schools in the U.S.; in addition, the trend has been *to increase* hours in recent years. This may be indicative of the Canadian emphasis on training family practitioners who will serve as generalists for all aspects of patient care. Departments of Family Practice are responsible for sexuality education in almost a third of Canadian medical schools, while this is true only in a minority of U.S. schools. The number of U.S. schools expanding sexuality class hours in recent years (28%) may also reflect a new emphasis in the United States on preparing primary care physicians.

While many medical schools devote class hours to sexuality, the timing of presentation of this material is of interest. The U.S. schools tend to concentrate these classes during the students' first or second year, generally a time frame in which students have little or no patient contact, and in which they are bombarded with basic science information. Without clinical experience, the more humanistic aspects of patient care (as exemplified by attending to sexuality issues) may appear less relevant to students. The majority of Canadian schools, on the other hand, present sexuality material after these preclinical years when the students are more advanced in their clinical training and have increased patient contact.

Both U.S. and Canadian medical schools appear to cover a wide range of sexuality topics. However, it seems unfortunate that some schools do not teach students sexual history taking or focus on issues of sex and disability/illness, since these are of vital importance for medical practitioners. Similarly, covering technical information on HIV/AIDS without devoting teaching time to the broader topics of homosexuality and bisexuality appears to neglect potentially important issues for medical practice.

Sexuality is an emotional charged area for the practitioner as well as for the patient. We believe that without specific training in sexual history taking, supervised experience in sex-related interviewing, and discussion of the sexual ramifications of illness, medical students will not develop important clinical skills and the necessary comfort to use these skills effectively in practice. For example, it will be even more difficult for the physician and a homosexual patient to be able to communicate effectively if the practitioner lacks information and understanding. The fact that schools in both the U.S. and Canada ignore these issues should be of concern to medical educators–and to the public.

Differences in presentation of sexuality material is another unresolved issue. In some schools, there is a separate sexuality course, in others, the material is offered as part of another specific course or clerkship. In some schools, the various departments involved do not seem to coordinate their teaching, perhaps resulting in some areas being neglected and others duplicated. It is not clear whether sexuality teaching is most effective when presented in a single block for maximum impact or when integrated throughout the curriculum in a variety of courses and clerkships. Studies are still needed to assess the factors of course timing, organization and integration.

Our survey presumably was completed primarily by the Deans of the various schools. Our data may reflect a tendency of administrators to overemphasize or underreport of the extent of sexuality teaching in their schools, for example, to include as class hours occasions when sexual topics were only superficially mentioned. Nonetheless, even if we arbitrarily eliminate schools offering less than six hours of class time–assuming that a greater number is suggestive of a more organized teaching approach–we still find 64% of U.S. and 92% of Canadian schools offering seven or more hours of sexuality education.

In previous decades, sexuality educators focused on two related approaches to medical sex education. On the one hand, students needed basic sex information to expand their knowledge. Of equal importance, it was believed, was to challenge attitudes and values, therefore, students were exposed to films/videos and panels of individuals whose life experiences reflected the spectrum of human sexual expression. It was assumed that this combination of knowledge acquisition and attitude reevaluation would develop a physician who was comfortable dealing with sexual issues in practice. Follow-up studies have focused on increased knowledge and attitude change after sexuality classes or courses (e.g., Garrard, Vaitkus, Held, & Chilgren, 1976; Lamberti & Chapel, 1977; Leif & Reed, 1972; Marcotte, Geyer, Kilpatrick, & Smith, 1976). However, as discussed by Schnarch and Jones (1981), short-term gains in learning may be lost over the course of medical education and may not help students develop the necessary skills to function effectively when they enter medical practice.

As North America has entered a more conservative era, some students may object to viewing sexually explicit materials and resent attempts to challenge their value systems. On the other hand, medical students of this generation have already been exposed to an explosion of sexual information, misinformation, and imagery from the media so that exposure to explicit material in a classroom setting may be less necessary even as a desensitizing medium. While we believe that a broad knowledge base is necessary for medical students, we are concerned that without significant emphasis and practice in sexual history taking, diagnosis of dysfunctions, and brief office counseling skills, the acquisition of information alone will not enable the utilization of this knowledge.

The existing data cannot resolve some key issues which remain to be addressed in future studies. It is vital that research focus on several important questions: (a) Is there a critical number of hours of sexuality instruction necessary to affect subsequent clinical practice patterns? (b) Do programs that focus on skill training have a more lasting impact on patient care than those that rely primarily on didactic material? (c) Is exposure to sexuality training more effective in changing subsequent practice when presented in preclinical or clinical years or both? (d) To what degree does sexuality training affect values and attitudes, and how important are any such changes to subsequent medical practice?

CONCLUSION

The primary care physician will continue to serve as a major resource and advisor for the vast majority of patients with sexual complaints. Therefore, the provision of adequate, effective training to prepare practitioners for this role continues as both the task and the challenge of contemporary medical education.

REFERENCES

Cross, R.J., Lief, H.I. & Lucas, V.C. (1984). Current trends in the sex education of medical students. Unpublished manuscript.

Garrard, V., Vaitkus, A., Held, V. & Chilgren, R.A. (1976). Follow-up effects of a medical school course in human sexuality. *Archives of Sexual Behavior*, *5*, 331-340.

Lamberti, V.W. & Chapel, V.L. (1977). Development and evaluation of a sex education program for medical students. *Journal of Medical Education*, *52*, 582-586.

Leif, H.I. & Reed, D.M. (1972). Sex knowledge and attitude test (SKAT). Center for the Study of Sex Education in Medicine, Department of Psychiatry, University of Pennsylvania, School of Medicine.

Lief, H.I. (1971). Sex education in medical schools. *Journal of Medical Education*, *46*, 372-374.

Lief, H.I. & Ebert, R.K. (1975). A survey of sex education in United States Medical Schools. *WHO Teaching Report, Education & Treatment in Human Sexuality: The Training of Health Professionals*, Series 572.

Lloyd, V.A. & Steinberger, K.E. (1977). Training in reproductive biology and human sexuality in American medical schools. *Journal of Medical Education*, *52*, 74-76.

Marcotte, D.B., Geyer, P.R., Kilpatrick, D.G. & Smith, A.D. (1976). The effect of a spaced sex education course on medical students' sexual knowledge and attitudes. *Medical Education*, *10*, 117-121.

Reader, F.C. (1994). Training in human sexuality in United Kingdom Medical Schools. *Sexual and Marital Therapy*, *9* (2), 193-200.

Schnarch, D.M. & Jones, K. (1981). Efficacy of sex education courses in medical schools. *Sex and Marital Therapy*, *7* (4), 307-317.

Index

References are indexed only when titles appear in text, and author names only when cited in full.

End-of-chapter Notes are selectively indexed: indicated by "n" preceded by page number and followed by Note number.

AASEC; AASECT 11,13
Abortion 5,16,42,100
Abstinence, sexual 38,88,93-94
Administrators, institutional:
    positions/support toward
    sexuality education issues
    12,72
  instructional methods
    73-74,77-80
  feminist perspectives educators
    and programs 53,55
  in seminary schools 168-170
  and student behavioral outcome
    evaluation related to 92
Adolescents. *See* children; *see under*
    Contraception
African Americans 38,39,81-82
Aged persons, sexuality of 40,44,50
AIDS. *See* HIV/AIDS
Allgeier, Elizabeth Rice 84
American Association of Colleges
    for Teacher Education
    (AACTE) 124
American Association of School
    Administrators 122
American Association of Sex
    Educators and Counselors
    (AASEC; AASECT) 11,13

American Society for Social and
    Moral Prophylaxis 6
Attitudes, values, and beliefs. *See*
    also Religious beliefs
  decision-making skills which
    incorporate 27-28
  existential bases of 18
  learning activities and subject
    matter contrary to, conflicts
    of 56,59,75,76-77,78,79-80,
    84,85
  in learning process, as essential
    component 88-92,96
  medical students' reevaluation
    and development 183
  self-assessment models
    73,166,167
  toward sexuality, by adolescents
    101
    and toward contraception use,
      implications of, and models
      for predicting 101-104
    and interventions for
      affecting attitude
      and behavioral
      changes 104-119
  traditional family values, threats
    to 16,91

For Product Safety Concerns and Information please contact our EU
representative GPSR@taylorandfrancis.com
Taylor & Francis Verlag GmbH, Kaufingerstraße 24, 80331 München, Germany

www.ingramcontent.com/pod-product-compliance
Ingram Content Group UK Ltd.
Pitfield, Milton Keynes, MK11 3LW, UK
UKHW021056080625
459435UK00003B/25